THE GAMBLING TIMES GUIDE TO

PLAYING GAMES
—— FOR ——
FUN AND PROFIT

By
Len Miller

An Original Gambling Times Edition
GAMBLING TIMES INCORPORATED
HOLLYWOOD, CALIFORNIA

Library of Congress Cataloging in Publication Data
MILLER, LEN
THE GAMBLING TIMES GUIDE TO
PLAYING GAMES FOR FUN AND PROFIT

ISBN: 0-89746-017-0

Manufactured in the United States of America
Printed and Bound by Kingsport Press

First Printing — January 1983

Cover by David McBride

All material presented in this book is offered as information to the reader. No inducement to gamble is intended or implied.

ACKNOWLEDGEMENTS

The author wishes to thank the following *Gambling Times* staff members for their help and assistance in producing this book: *Arnold L. Abrams*—Executive Production Manager, Book Division; *Jerrold Kazdoy*—Editorial Production Manager, Book Division; *Joanne Gutreimen*—Editorial Researcher; and *David B. James* and *Andrea Pollock*—Composition.

TABLE OF CONTENTS

PREFACE

Before we discuss the individual casino games we play for fun and profit, I would like to introduce you to casino gaming in general.

In my years as editor of *Gambling Times* magazine, I have had the opportunity to visit all of the casinos in Atlantic City, Las Vegas, Reno, and Lake Tahoe, in addition to other gaming areas.

Without slighting the glamour, beauty, and historical background of the European casinos that I have also visited, I must say that the American casinos provide the best possible atmosphere for the player.

It is simple and easy to play at any of the casino tables here: the milieu is more informal, and one can enter and leave a game at will. If you have winning chips to cash in, the attendants at the cashiers cage count your chips and pay you in cash, with a smile. If you win a large amount of money, you will be offered the courtesy of a safety deposit box, or the casino cashier will give you a receipt for as much money as you wish to leave for safekeeping.

By and large, the casinos extend a good deal of courtesy and respect to the players. If you are a big player you may receive complimentary dinners, show reservations, and even hotel accommodations. Almost all of the casinos, small and large alike, serve complimentary drinks to the players. (A word of advice here: Although you are obviously at a casino-resort hotel for a good time, it would be wise to confine your drinking to after you've finished playing and have left the tables.)

Without question, these resorts provide the very best in outdoor and indoor amenities. Swimming pools, tennis courts, golf courses, and even bowling are available to vacationers. Most holiday-seekers combine these fun activities into their schedule. The superior quality and diversity of entertainment offered in each hotel is scarcely available anywhere else in the world. Food is also lavishly offered in a number of dining areas, including coffee shops, buffets, and gourmet restaurants. There definitely is something for everyone's taste in these beautiful casino-resort complexes.

Of course, we all agree that it's the casinos' gambling profits that pay for all of this. But, some people *do* win and that is why you are reading this book. You can be one of those who walk away from the casino with profits to take home. When you do, you'll be among the 10% or so who do win. That's just fine with the casinos—they like those percentages: 90% losers, 10% winners.

In all fairness, though, the casinos are not responsible for anyone losing. All the casinos do is provide a beautiful game floor with the various games attended by dealers. They admittedly have a built-in advantage, a percentage in their favor. Those percentages may not be known to most of the players but, luckily for you, these figures will become part of your overall knowledge. Possessing this information will give you a decided edge over those 90% of the people who lose enough to pay for all the overhead in the casinos and provide a tidy profit for management.

Let me stress that learning the right way to play casino games is much the same as learning how to play bridge, chess, backgammon or even how to properly hold a tennis racket. There is no sure way of winning all of the time, and there definitely is an element of luck and timing involved in most of the games, but there is also a *right* way to play each game.

Your attitude is all-important in becoming a winning player. In fact, your attitude sets the stage for how well you accept and follow the principles set forth in this book. Obviously, some people can read the same text and get more out of what they read and learn than others reading the same material.

Casino games are fun and exciting to play. Competition is the key word, especially when you've got your money on the line against the adversary: the casino. You are now going to learn to compete against the table at whatever game you're playing. The competition ends when you walk away from the game; let's see if we can make you a winner most of those times.

FOREWORD

In any sporting game such as tennis, golf, bowling, etc., a good part of winning lies in strength, endurance, and other forms of physical prowess. Yet, even in those games, a good part of winning also has to do with awareness, psychological advantage, being sharp, and looking for an edge.

In more passive games such as bridge, chess, backgammon, gin rummy and poker, physical attributes are not that important. In fact, the most needed physical qualifications are to be well rested and mentally alert.

In those card games just mentioned, skill is the main requirement for winning. Becoming a better player in any game, and then expanding that expertise each time you play or practice, is the best winning formula I know of.

The games discussed in this "how-to" manual are available in the gaming casinos in Nevada, Atlantic City, and throughout the world.

Over the past few years, readers of *Gambling Times* magazine have learned that there are better ways to play *any* game. By playing *better*, the gamer has a greater chance of winning more, and losing less. *That in effect is the crux of the entire matter.* Becoming a more knowledgeable player of any game gives one a feeling of confidence that contributes to winning.

Learning the rules and procedures of playing each game, and becoming totally conversant with those regulations, is the first important step. I can hardly think of anyone disagreeing with that statement. And yet, a large percentage of casino players are not totally familiar with the rules and procedures of the games they play. Once you have mastered these prerequisites, you'll find that playing the games becomes pleasant, entertaining and fun!

So there you have it. When you finish reading this book, you'll be able to enjoy your gaming sojourns better than ever. Best of all, it's yours to read over again and to keep as a handy source of reference.

Yours for winning,

Len Miller

Chapter 5
<u>Roulette</u>: Learning the Wheel and the Betting Layout

Roulette is one of the oldest games in the casino. In fact, it is the most popular of the casino games throughout Europe. Without question it's a game of fun, and with a little knowledge and practice, it can be profitable as well.

Roulette is strictly a game of chance. But, notwithstanding the element of luck involved, there are ways to play the roulette wheel that can enhance your lucky streak and enable you to win progressively larger amounts as your luck continues. In this chapter, we will discuss these methods and betting systems.

The Spinning Wheel

First, let's examine both the wheel and the betting table layout so that you can fully understand all of the bets and procedures in playing roulette.

The roulette wheel is divided into 38 numbered slots, including the numbers 1 through 36 and then a 0 and a 00. In Europe there is only a single 0, and only 37 numbered slots to the wheel. A single-0 wheel can also be found in certain selected casinos in Nevada and Atlantic City.

The house advantage is that with both 0 and 00, the player receives odds payoff of 35 to 1, rather than the true odds of 37 to 1. That house advantage amounts to 5.6% and that is how the casinos earn their money. Ostensibly they make $5.60 on every $100 wagered. The European wheel with its single 0 has a house advantage of just 2.7%; they would make $2.70 on every $100 wagered at the roulette table.

In either case, a house rake of 2.7% to a fraction over 5% is not too bad of an edge to combat. By comparison, thoroughbred race tracks take 17% to 20% for their cut.

All of the wheels in Nevada and Atlantic City have the same sequence of numbers spread around the wheel. The table layout is also the same. So, wherever you play, the rules and regulations will be familiar to you.

Getting Acquainted

Roulette is played at a table that seats six to seven players. Each player is assigned a particular colored chip which remains with that player until he or she leaves the game. Those chips must be cashed in at the roulette table—they do not have value at any other table or at the cashiers cage.

Also, each player may be playing for different stakes. The value of each player's colored chips is set by the player. If a player enters the game by asking for a stack of fifty-cent chips, the dealer will hand over a stack of 40 chips, all the same color, and receive $20; for those wishing to play with twenty-five-cent chips, a $20 bill will get them 80 chips. In order to determine the amount of each player's chips, the dealer places one of the colored chips on the rim of the wheel with a price marker on top of that chip. With up to seven players placing bets all over the table, the colored chips quickly identify each player and the dealer makes the proper payoffs quickly and efficiently.

When large amounts are won by the players, the dealer may elect to pay off with regular casino chips of $5 and $25 value. For example, if a player bet two fifty-cent chips on a single number and won, the payoff would be either 70 of the colored chips or $35 in $5 chips. If a player is winning, you'll usually see casino chips and the colored roulette chips stacked up in front of that player.

In Diagram 5-1, we see the betting table layout, with the circled letters designating each type of bet that may be made; Table 5-1 explains each of these bets and their odds payoffs.

Placing Bets

In most casinos the roulette table has a small sign stating the minimum bet per spin. It's usually a $2 minimum bet: that means $2 in accumulative bets, not one bet for $2. For example, if you're

Diagram 5-1

playing with fifty-cent chips you can put one chip on a single number, another chip on a two-number split bet, and two chips on red. Thus, if your single number or two-number bet loses, but the winning number was red, you'd win two chips on the red bet, and lose the other two bets if they didn't hit. In most cases you'll be betting more than four chips, so you'll make the minimum bet qualification.

The wheel has exactly 18 red numbers and 18 black numbers, with the 0 and 00 colored green. There is only one bad bet on the board: that is the "E" bet of five numbers—0, 00, 1, 2, 3. In all other bets, whether they're single-number bets, groups, red, black, dozens, columns, etc., the house edge remains at 5.6%.

After the player places his bet(s) on the betting layout, the dealer spins the wheel and then rolls the ball in the opposite direction along the top inner edge of the wheel. As the ball slows down it loses force, bounces around the slotted wheel and finally settles in one of the 38 numbered slots. That number is the declared winner.

The dealer places a marker on that particular number so that all of the players can see the results of that spin. The dealer then pays off each player who had a bet on that number or a bet on any related payoff. For example, if the winning number was 17, the following payoffs would be made:

First of all, all bets on the single number 17 would receive 35

Table 5-1

The chips used in roulette are colored for identification only... You set their value when you buy a stack. Using chips or coins, bets are placed on the roulette layout as shown in Diagram 5-1. There are red and black numbered squares from number one to number 36. These numbers are divided into three groups: first 12, second 12, and third 12. They are also divided for betting purposes into three horizontal groups (see the diagram) from 3 to 36, 2 to 35, and 1 to 34. Bets may also be placed on groups of numbers from 1 to 18, and 19 to 36. Also shown in the diagram are 0 and 00. These are colored green.

Betting may also be made on odd or even numbers or on red and black numbers as the dealer spins the ball. The payoff for roulette bets is as follows (see the diagram for position):

If the ball lands in...

A Red or black or 1-18 or 19-36 . . . . even money
B Groups of 12 numbers (dozens) . . . . 2 to 1
A Odd or even . . . . even money
B Groups of 12 numbers (columns) . . . . . . 2 to 1
C Any one number or 0 or 00 . . . . 35 to 1

SPLIT BETS

D Any one of the six in the group . . . . 5 to 1
E 0, 00, 1, 2 or 3 . . . . 6 to 1
F Any one of the four in a group . . . . 8 to 1
G Any one of the three in a group . . . . 11 to 1
H Any one of the two numbers . . . . 17 to 1
I 0 or 00 . . . . .17 to 1

chips for each chip bet. Number 17 is red, which would give all red bets an even money payoff. It is also in the 1 to 18 range and a bet there gets even money. It's in the second dozen, which gives a 2 to 1 payoff, and also in the middle column, and a bet there gets paid off at 2 to 1. It's an odd-bet win too.

Betting Blocks

There's another way to select numbers and for this choice we look at the wheel in Diagram 5-2. You will note that the numbers are placed around the wheel not in 1-2-3 order, but in another manner. The red 1 is exactly opposite the black 2. The green 00 is opposite the green 0. It continues until we find black 35 opposite red 36.

Diagram 5–2

Many roulette players, those who follow systems especially, play blocks of numbers as seen on the wheel. Here is an example of that method, or system, of betting.

This method requires five chips. Place one chip on a six-number bet, as shown by "D" in Diagram 5-1. Let's say you select the block of six numbers, 10 through 15. Your one chip would be placed on the line between the 10 and 13; this signifies a six-number bet covering 10, 11, 12, 13, 14, 15.

Now take four chips and place one each on 16, 17, 18 and 28. This will give you a total of 10 numbers covered with five chips. You'll notice that, as shown in Diagram 5-2, your 10 numbers are spread around the wheel so that each number is no more than three spaces apart, and in some cases only two numbered slots from each other. When the ball bounces around the wheel, it has a good chance of landing in one of the slots within the numbers you selected.

If one of your six-number group wins, you'll receive five chips to your one-chip bet. Naturally, you will lose the other four chips you bet on the single numbers. But you now have six chips, one more than the five you started with. After such a win, you should now increase your six-number bet to two chips, keeping the same bet of one chip on each of the four single numbers. If you hit one of the four numbers, you'll get a payoff of 35 chips, giving you a win of 36 chips—less the five chips invested—for a net win of 31 chips. When this happens, double all bets. If you are lucky enough to win the third time in a row, double all bets again. This is called *progressive win betting*. Remember: You *never* increase your bets on losses, but only on wins.

Take the time to read this chapter over again, so that you can become completely conversant with the game of roulette. Then plan your strategy of betting single numbers and groups so that the next time the wheel spins, you'll be playing roulette for fun as well as profit.

Roulette Terminology

BLACK—A roulette bet on all the black numbers. Pays 1 to 1.

BLOCK BETTING—The set of numbers on one section of the wheel which are bet *en masse* in certain roulette strategies.

COLUMN BET—A bet on an entire column of numbers; there are three available columns. Pays 2 to 1.

CORNER BET—A roulette four-number bet. Pays 8 to 1.

COUP—One roll; one decision. Winning bet.

DEALER—The casino employee who conducts the roulette wheel.

DOUBLE-ZERO—A bet on the 38th number on the wheel, colored green. Pays 35 to 1, as any other *straight* bet.

DOZENS BET—A bet on any of the three available groups of 12 numbers. Either 1 through 12, 13 through 24, or 25 through 36. Pays 2 to 1.

EVEN—A bet on all of the 18 even numbers. Pays 1 to 1.

GREEN NUMBERS—The zero and double-zero.

HIGH or LOW—A bet on either the first 18 numbers (Low: 1–18) or the second 18 (High: 19–36). Pays 1 to 1.

HOUSE PERCENTAGE—The advantage the casino has over the player. In American roulette, it's 5.26%.

INSIDE BET—Any bet made on numbers directly inside the layout. Odds for winning inside bets range from 5 to 1, up to 35 to 1.

LINE BET—A bet on any six adjoining numbers. Pays 5 to 1.

NEIGHBORS—The numbers immediately to the left and right of the winning number.

19–36—A bet on the second half of the numbers in the layout. Pays 1 to 1.

ODD—A bet on all of the odd numbers. Pays 1 to 1.

1–18—A bet on the first half of the numbers on the wheel. Pays 1 to 1.

OUTSIDE BET—The betting area on the roulette table bordering the numbers layout. This includes columns, dozens, black-red, odd-even, 1–18, 19–36. Pays 1 to 1.

PIT BOSS—Supervisor in charge of the roulette wheel.

PROGRESSIVE BETTING—To build up a bet by placing your winnings from the previous bet on top of your current bet.

RED—A roulette bet on all the red numbers. Pays 1 to 1.

RUN—Series of like results, such as four red or six odd.

SINGLE NUMBER—A roulette straight-up bet. Pays 35 to 1.

SIX-LINE BET—A roulette six-number bet. Pays 5 to 1.

SLOTS—Sections of the roulette wheel which hold the numbers.

SPECIAL LINE BET—A bet on the first five numbers: 0,00,1,2 and 3 *only*. Pays 6 to 1.

SPLIT BET—A bet on any two adjoining numbers. Pays 17 to 1.

SQUARE/QUARTER BET—A bet on any four numbers in a square. Pays 8 to 1.

STRAIGHT BET—A bet on any one number. Pays 35 to 1.

STREET BET—A bet on any three numbers in a line. Pays 11 to 1.

TOKE—Gratuity or tip for the dealer.

WHEEL CHECKS—The special unmarked chips that are used specifically on roulette tables.

ZERO—A bet on the 37th number on the wheel; colored green. Pays 35 to 1, as any other *straight* bet.

Chapter 6
<u>Keno</u>:
Upping
Your Chances

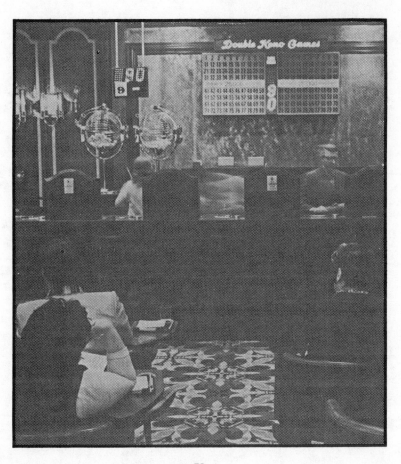

As any frequent visitor to Las Vegas knows, one of the most enduring and popular diversions in the Strip hotels and the downtown casinos is the game of keno. Keno is enjoyed for many reasons: It's simple to play, requires no particular skill to win big, and can be played in a leisurely fashion. Whether you're enjoying a sumptuous meal in the hotel restaurant, relaxing in the keno lounge with a cool drink, or standing in the glamorous casino lobby, you'll find the keno numbers are visible from practically anywhere in the hotel. Busy keno writers constantly make the rounds from the restaurant to the keno lounge and through the hotel lobby to dispense winnings and pick up new playing tickets. Simply put, keno is a fascinating game of chance.

The Origins of Keno

Keno today, with its automatic "goose" through which ping-pong balls printed with the keno numbers are electrically popped, is not the modern game one might assume it is. Actually, keno dates back to the Chinese Han dynasty, preceding our current version by nearly 2000 years. The game was originally introduced to the public by a man named Cheung Leung, who devised it as a way for the Chinese government to raise much-needed revenues for their army. Originally, 120 different Chinese ideograph characters were used to place bets, but this number was eventually reduced to 90. The people took to it immediately, making it a smashing success which netted loads of cash for the state. And to this day, keno has enjoyed unflagging popularity.

In the gay nineties, when Chinese immigrants brought the game with them to the United States, the 90 characters were further reduced to 80. The game soon garnered favor with Americans, who nevertheless found the Chinese ideograph characters hard to differentiate. To facilitate their play, the Chinese characters were replaced by ordinary Arabic numerals from one to 80. If you pick up a keno ticket today, you will see it is still numbered from one to 80.

A few other changes have been made. Originally, wooden balls with the keno numbers on them were pulled by hand through a wooden "goose" neck. Nowadays, lightweight ping-pong balls are used, and they are not manually moved; it's all done by machinery to ensure ease and fairness. The balls are forced aerodynamically through the "goose" and then pop up, revealing the numbers for that game. The numbers appear on an electrically lighted board in the lobby, the hotel restaurant or, for that matter, almost any place in the casino where one would get the urge to take a chance!

Originally, keno was introduced in Nevada as "race-horse keno," in which each ball popped up bearing not only a number but the name of a race horse. This "race-horse" aspect was dropped from the game in 1951, when the Nevada government passed a bill taxing off-track betting. So, for the past 31 years, it's been strictly a numbers game.

Playing the Game

While sitting in the keno lounge and sipping a drink, you can fill out a paper keno ticket for the low price of 70 cents, using the special black crayon provided, and watch the keno numbers light up on the board over the dealers' station. Although this is not the only locale in the casino where one can play, it's fun to sit in the special keno combination desk-chairs (which are a bit like the kind in old school houses, except with a convenient compartment for your drink), while cheerful, attractive keno writers are at your beck and call. This is perhaps the only big advantage keno has over the other games in the casino: it can be played in a completely relaxed atmosphere, without the dizzying adrenalin rush that so characterizes many of the table games. It's one of the reasons why keno is such a big favorite with novice bettors and recreational players.

A fascinating aspect of keno is that it is seemingly all dependent on chance, with absolutely no way for anybody to predict which numbers will surface in any given game. But there are definitely aspects of the game that you should consider before plunking down your quarters and dimes for a keno ticket. These aspects could very well give you an edge over the average, non-strategic *straight* keno bettor.

The keno ticket is played by marking off, with circles or X's, anywhere from one to 15 numbers on a ticket. The payoff on a *straight* bet will be determined by what percentage of your numbers comes up out of the ones that you bet. The minimum price of the keno ticket is usually 70 cents; a higher ticket price, of course, will get you bigger stakes. You give your ticket to the keno writer, for which you'll receive a marked-up duplicate which is stamped with the ticket number, date and game played. This is your receipt. Then, all you do is wait for your numbers to light up!

If you do win a keno game by having a number or numbers light up, you *must* present your ticket to collect your winnings—either to a keno writer or to the dealer directly—before the start of the next game. If you're too tardy in presenting your receipt, your chance to collect will be gone! So, please be prompt.

Betting...By the Numbers

If you take the time to scrutinize the payoff sheet, you'll see that the winnings really skyrocket as the proportion of the numbers chosen that come up grows. If you're playing, for example, eight spots for $1.40 and five numbers come up, that nets you a win of $12, which is a payoff of about 8 for 1. But when you're only playing five numbers, getting all five means you rake in $680—a 485 to 1 payoff—for the same ticket price!

By looking at these stakes, one might assume that it's best to play few numbers, rather than many, on a *straight* ticket. Is this necessarily so? Well, it all depends on what kind of a player you are. Remember that the house edge in the game of keno is astronomical, probably higher than that of most other games. Some players figure that, taking these high odds into consideration, they might as well play a long-shot game with just a few numbers each time, keeping their fingers crossed and hoping for a miracle. Other bettors play a high or maximum number of spots to increase their chances of having a win, and are content with a much smaller kitty. For example, if the same five spots we mentioned earlier had come up on a ticket on which 10 numbers had been played for $1.40, the payoff would have been only $2.80—not a killing, certainly, but still enough to play two or three more games and have some fun.

Ways to Play

So far, we've only discussed the *straight* ticket which, for one price, gives you one shot at one group of numbers. There is, however, a much more sophisticated way of playing keno which, for a slightly higher initial price, gives you a much better shot at picking up some winnings. This is to bet either a *way* or *combination* ticket.

With a *way* keno bet, your ticket is marked with three or more equal groups of numbers, bringing your ticket price to the number of groups times the amount you're playing; that is, playing three groups of numbers at 70 cents will cost you a total of $2.10. It is a bit more expensive to play this way, so you can't play as many games as you could if you were to just bet 70-cent *straight* tickets all night.

But remember, keno is a game which should only be played for short stretches of time anyhow, since it's impossible to buck the gigantic house edge over any length of time. And with a *way* ticket, you're much more assured of some kind of shot at a win. If, for example, you mark off three groups of four numbers, you can collect on three eight-spot bets, three four-spot bets, and the total twelve-spot bet, making the ticket price $4.90 but giving you lots of chances to win on just one ticket. Considering all the factors, it's a lot smarter to play this way than to repeatedly take your chances with a one-shot *straight* ticket. Just make sure to clearly mark, on the right-hand margin of your keno ticket, the type of bet you are taking.

Now we come to the *combination* ticket. On this type of bet, you can have groups of numbers of different count—say, two fours and a two—and bet on the different combinations. On a four, four and two-spot, one might bet on the one two-spot, both four-spots, the two different four-and-two (6) combinations, one eight-spot (the four-and-four), and also play the ticket as a total 10-spot. This gives you a great range of winnings that can come up, again, for a price of $4.90. Remember, too, that this is about the only way of playing that can give you a decent shot at the big stakes.

Compare this type of wager with the more common *straight* ticket. If you chose 12 spots, for example, on a 70-cent *straight* ticket, an eight out of 12 win would net you $150. But the same eight numerals coming up on one eight-spot *way* of a *combination* ticket will hand you a jackpot of $12,500. The smaller wins are all possible too, of course, but with the odds this high, always think in terms of a big score. Because the keno odds are so huge in favor of the house, the smart player will use his head and make each ticket really worthwhile.

The Numbers Game

Choosing which numbers to play is a personal, somewhat mystical ritual. It seems remarkable, sometimes, how certain people can invest certain numbers with a strongly directed personal force and almost "will" the numbers to appear. Many people have standard "lucky numbers" that seem to come in for them more often than not. Others will play the number of children that they have, or grandchildren, or the date of Baby's birthday, or perhaps an anniversary number.

Some canny players watch the games for a few hours without placing any bets, and write down the numbers that seem to be recurring frequently. There are two schools of thought on how to handle these commonly-seen numbers. One method is to favor these particular numbers when making your bets, since if they've been coming up regularly, there's no real reason they should stop. Perhaps there is a physical reason for this, as well: these common-show numbers may appear often because the balls holding the other numbers may be scratched or damaged in some way, and not as likely to pop up into the "goose." (But, then again, there is the theory that one should definitely play the numerals that haven't been seen in quite a while, since, according to the law of averages, they're "due" to make a showing.)

To summarize, then, the best method of playing keno is to opt for the *way* or *combination* tickets, using a pool of numbers drawn from your own personal favorites, the ones commonly seen that day, and perhaps one or two digits you haven't seen in a while. Then order a drink, relax, and get ready to win!

* * *

The following charts, illustrations, and instructions for playing keno are presented here through the courtesy of the Sands Hotel on the Strip in Las Vegas.

HOW TO PLAY

MARK SPOTS

Mark your spots' by crossing out eight numbers with a heavy X. These numbers can be chosen from any of the 80 numbers on the blank ticket. Write the price — 1.00 —in the square located at the upper right hand corner of the ticket. **Crayons and blank tickets are conveniently located throughout the club.** (Any multiple of 1.00 may be played — 5.00 — 10.00.) 2.00 minimum bet on 11 thru 15 spot tickets.

HAND TICKET IN

Give your ticket, along with the amount of your wager to any of our friendly Keno dealers. You will receive a copy of your ticket marked on an authorized copy with the next game number located in the upper right hand corner. This game number is for the next drawing of numbers. **Remember, your ticket is good for that game only!** You may use that ticket to "replay" the same numbers again on a later game; this saves you the trouble of marking a new blank.

DETERMINE YOUR CATCH

Twenty numbers of the 80 are automatically chosen. These numbers are called out over the public address system and lit on the Keno flash boards located throughout the hotel. Compare your tickets with the numbers that are lit, if five or more match the numbers you have chosen **YOU HAVE A WINNER! Present your ticket to any Keno dealer for payment before the start of the next game.** For your added convenience, special Keno tickets with the winning numbers are distributed throughout the club. Place one of these "DRAWS" with the corresponding game number over your ticket to determine the catch. **GOOD LUCK!**

it's as easy as one-two-three

1 MARK SPOTS

2 HAND TICKET IN

3 DETERMINE YOUR CATCH

RULES

PLEASE CHECK YOUR TICKET.
Corrections must be made before start of next game or the ticket you receive will be ruled valid and accepted as issued.

KENO RUNNERS ARE FOR YOUR CONVENIENCE.
We cannot be responsible if tickets are too late for the current game.

TOTAL AGGREGATE PAYOUT PER GAME IS $50,000.00
to all players participating in the game.

WINNING TICKETS MUST BE CASHED
immediately after each game is called and before the start of the next game.

REMEMBER
Avoid being shut out. Play your tickets early for the next game and also remember, you may play as many tickets as you desire on each game...the more wagered on each ticket, the smaller the catch needed to win the $50,000.00 limit.

1 SPOT • Pick One Number

CATCH	BET $1.00	BET $5.00	BET $10.00
1 WIN	3.00	15.00	30.00

2 SPOTS • Pick Two Numbers

CATCH	BET $1.00	BET $5.00	BET $10.00
2 WIN	12.00	60.00	120.00

3 SPOTS • Pick Three Numbers

CATCH	BET $1.00	BET $5.00	BET $10.00
2 WIN	1.00	5.00	10.00
3 WIN	42.00	210.00	420.00

SPECIAL TICKETS NOW AVAILABLE
ON
4 SPOT THRU 9 SPOT

★ Please mark SPECIAL TICKETS ·'SP'· ★

All Tickets will be paid at the regular
S1 Rate unless marked ·'SPECIAL'·

SPECIAL TICKETS 4 SPOT THRU 9 SPOT

REGULAR

CATCH	BET $1.00	BET $5.00	BET $10.00
2 WIN	1.00	5.00	10.00
3 WIN	4.00	20.00	40.00
4 WIN	112.00	560.00	1,120.00

4 SPOTS • Pick Four Numbers   SPECIAL*

CATCH	BET $1.00	BET $5.00	BET $10.00
3 WIN	2.00	10.00	20.00
4 WIN	200.00	1,000.00	2,000.00

REGULAR

CATCH	BET $1.00	BET $5.00	BET $10.00
3 WIN	2.00	10.00	20.00
4 WIN	20.00	100.00	200.00
5 WIN	480.00	2,400.00	4,800.00

5 SPOTS • Pick Five Numbers   SPECIAL*

CATCH	BET $1.00	BET $5.00	BET $10.00
3 WIN	1.00	5.00	10.00
4 WIN	14.00	70.00	140.00
5 WIN	700.00	3,500.00	7,000.00

		REGULAR	
CATCH	BET $1.00	BET $5.00	BET $10.00
3 WIN	1.00	5.00	10.00
4 WIN	4.00	20.00	40.00
5 WIN	88.00	440.00	880.00
6 WIN	1,500.00	7,500.00	15,000.00

6 SPOTS • Pick Six Numbers — SPECIAL✳

CATCH	BET $1.00	BET $5.00	BET $10.00
3 WIN	.50	2.50	5.00
4 WIN	2.50	12.50	25.00
5 WIN	90.00	450.00	900.00
6 WIN	2,270.00	11,350.00	22,700.00

		REGULAR	
CATCH	BET $1.00	BET $5.00	BET $10.00
4 WIN	2.00	10.00	20.00
5 WIN	24.00	120.00	240.00
6 WIN	360.00	1,800.00	3,600.00
7 WIN	5,000.00	25,000.00	50,000.00

7 SPOTS • Pick Seven Numbers — SPECIAL✳

CATCH	BET $1.00	BET $5.00	BET $10.00
4 WIN	1.00	5.00	10.00
5 WIN	16.00	80.00	160.00
6 WIN	420.00	2,100.00	4,200.00
7 WIN	8,200.00	41,000.00	50,000.00

REGULAR

CATCH	BET $1.00	BET $5.00	BET $10.00
5 WIN	9.00	45.00	90.00
6 WIN	90.00	450.00	900.00
7 WIN	1,500.00	7,500.00	15,000.00
8 WIN	19,000.00	**50,000.00**	**50,000.00**

8 SPOTS • Pick Eight Numbers   **SPECIAL⁎**

CATCH	BET $1.00	BET $5.00	BET $10.00
5 WIN	5.00	25.00	50.00
6 WIN	75.00	375.00	750.00
7 WIN	2,000.00	10,000.00	20,000.00
8 WIN	25,000.00	**50,000.00**	**50,000.00**

REGULAR

CATCH	BET $1.00	BET $5.00	BET $10.00
5 WIN	4.00	20.00	40.00
6 WIN	44.00	220.00	440.00
7 WIN	300.00	1,500.00	3,000.00
8 WIN	4,000.00	20,000.00	**40,000.00**
9 WIN	20,000.00	**50,000.00**	**50,000.00**

9 SPOTS • Pick Nine Numbers   **SPECIAL⁎**

CATCH	BET $1.00	BET $5.00	BET $10.00
5 WIN	3.00	15.00	30.00
6 WIN	42.00	210.00	420.00
7 WIN	300.00	1,500.00	3,000.00
8 WIN	4,800.00	24,000.00	**48,000.00**
9 WIN	25,000.00	**50,000.00**	**50,000.00**

10 SPOTS • Pick Ten Numbers

CATCH	BET $1.00	BET $5.00	BET $10.00
5 WIN	2.00	10.00	20.00
6 WIN	20.00	100.00	200.00
7 WIN	132.00	660.00	1,320.00
8 WIN	960.00	4,800.00	9,600.00
9 WIN	3,800.00	19,000.00	38,000.00
10 WIN	25,000.00	50,000.00	50,000.00

11 SPOTS • Pick Eleven Numbers $2.00 Minimum

CATCH	BET $2.00	BET $5.00	BET $10.00
5 WIN	2.00	5.00	10.00
6 WIN	16.00	40.00	80.00
7 WIN	144.00	360.00	720.00
8 WIN	720.00	1,800.00	3,600.00
9 WIN	3,600.00	9,000.00	18,000.00
10 WIN	24,000.00	50,000.00	50,000.00
11 WIN	50,000.00	50,000.00	50,000.00

12 SPOTS • Pick Twelve Numbers $2.00 Minimum

CATCH	BET $2.00	BET $5.00	BET $10.00
6 WIN	10.00	25.00	50.00
7 WIN	64.00	160.00	320.00
8 WIN	480.00	1,200.00	2,400.00
9 WIN	1,200.00	3,000.00	6,000.00
10 WIN	3,200.00	8,000.00	16,000.00
11 WIN	24,000.00	50,000.00	50,000.00
12 WIN	50,000.00	50,000.00	50,000.00

13 SPOTS • Pick Thirteen Numbers $2.00 Minimum

CATCH	BET $2.00	BET $5.00	BET $10.00
6 WIN	2.00	5.00	10.00
7 WIN	32.00	80.00	160.00
8 WIN	160.00	400.00	800.00
9 WIN	1,440.00	3,600.00	7,200.00
10 WIN	8,000.00	20,000.00	40,000.00
11 WIN	16,000.00	40,000.00	50,000.00
12 WIN	40,000.00	50,000.00	50,000.00
13 WIN	50,000.00	50,000.00	50,000.00

14 SPOTS • Pick Fourteen Numbers $2.00 Minimum

CATCH	BET $2.00	BET $5.00	BET $10.00
6 WIN	2.00	5.00	10.00
7 WIN	20.00	50.00	100.00
8 WIN	80.00	200.00	400.00
9 WIN	640.00	1,600.00	3,200.00
10 WIN	2,000.00	5,000.00	10,000.00
11 WIN	6,400.00	16,000.00	32,000.00
12 WIN	32,000.00	50,000.00	50,000.00
13 WIN	50,000.00	50,000.00	50,000.00
14 WIN	50,000.00	50,000.00	50,000.00

15 SPOTS • Pick Fifteen Numbers $2.00 Minimum

CATCH	BET $2.00	BET $5.00	BET $10.00
7 WIN	16.00	40.00	80.00
8 WIN	56.00	140.00	280.00
9 WIN	264.00	660.00	1,320.00
10 WIN	600.00	1,500.00	3,000.00
11 WIN	5,200.00	13,000.00	26,000.00
12 WIN	16,000.00	40,000.00	50,000.00
13 WIN	50,000.00	50,000.00	50,000.00
14 WIN	50,000.00	50,000.00	50,000.00
15 WIN	50,000.00	50,000.00	50,000.00

Play Keno in our
Comfortable Keno Lounge
or in the
Regency Lounge, Garden Room
Casino Area and all Bars

Keno Runners — another special service —
are available at all the above locations

You will find KENO tickets available in most dining areas and lounges throughout the SANDS. Simply mark your tickets and ask any employee to have a KENO runner sent to you.

You may then sit back and enjoy yourself, watching the results on one of the many lighted KENO boards installed for your convenience.

Please remember that the KENO runner must take your ticket to the master KENO marking area to have it validated. Have your tickets ready as early as possible. We cannot accept responsibility for tickets that are turned in too late for the succeeding game.

Keno Terminology

COMBINATION TICKET—A keno ticket on which several groups of numbers are played.

GOOSE—The clear plastic apparatus through which the modern keno balls are aerodynamically propelled. In the past, the goose was made of wood.

KENO WRITERS—The people who comb the casino, collecting keno tickets and delivering winnings. The same term applies to those who write tickets behind the counter.

KING TICKET—A keno ticket on which one (king) number is used to pair up with groups of numbers.

RACE-HORSE KENO—A previously-played form of keno in which each ball was imprinted with the name of a race horse as well as a number.

STRAIGHT TICKET—A keno ticket which is played as one set of numbers.

WAY TICKET—The same as a *combination ticket*.

Chapter 7
<u>Poker</u>: The People's Choice

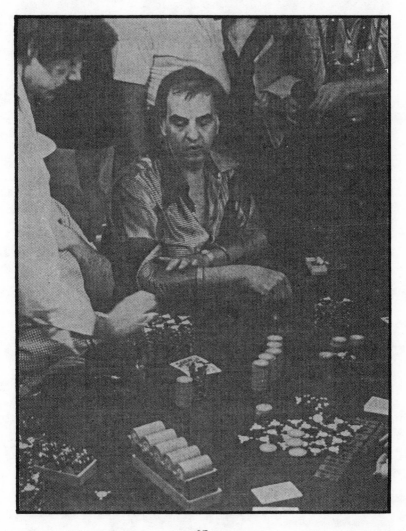

Poker has been, and continues to be, one of the most popular of all the social card games. Although we have other popular card games, such as bridge (which is played widely across the nation, and even abroad), gin rummy, hearts and pinochle, poker continues to be the best kind of gambling card game.

It's estimated that there are over 20 million serious-minded poker players throughout the United States. These are people who play regularly in a weekly game, usually with the same friendly group. They play at home, in social and country clubs, or in the various business service organizations.

Mapping It Out

Poker is very popular throughout the state of Nevada, where gambling is legal. There are poker rooms in most of the casinos, and various styles of the game are played. Stakes go anywhere from as small as $1 to $3 bets, up to $15 and $30, $50 and $100, and, in some places, no-limit stakes where pots may reach as high as $100,000.

California also has legalized poker; these games are played in card clubs scattered throughout the state. Some smaller card rooms have two or three tables, others have six to 10, and then there are the larger clubs. Gardena, a small Southern California municipality just 20 minutes from downtown Los Angeles, has six modern card clubs, much like the ones in the Las Vegas casinos. "The Bell Club" is also in close proximity. Located in Bell, California, a suburb of Los Angeles, this card club has more poker tables than *any* other establishment in the world. There are also a number of card clubs in San Diego and the surrounding area.

In Northern California you'll find card clubs in the San Francisco Bay area, Stockton, Palo Alto, San Jose, Sacramento, Redding, Santa Clara, and many other towns and cities.

With all the card clubs throughout the state, there is probably more card-playing going on in California than in any other state, with the exception of Nevada.

The state of Iowa has no card rooms as such. However, there are two types of social gambling licenses available: One is for beer and liquor establishments, and the other is for social and public places such as senior citizen and community centers. They have rules governing the amount of the wager permitted in their poker games. Wagers are limited to a $50 maximum; that is, no participant can win or lose more than $50 in any 24-hour period. Of course, these rules are subject to change; as time goes on, they may become more liberalized.

Oregon also has guidelines for their card clubs: No one can win or lose more than $10 in any four-hour span. These games are strictly social, but extremely popular in many places.

Montana offers municipalities the option of voting in favor of licensed card rooms. As a result, card rooms are legal in almost every city in Montana, including Billings, Bozeman, Butte, Great Falls and Helena.

The state of Washington also offers municipalities the option of voting for licensed card rooms in their areas, like Vancouver, Spokane, Seattle, Olympia and Yacama.

There is good reason to believe that with the proliferation of poker tournaments, and with more and more people playing poker, we may soon find legalized card rooms in other areas as well.

What's The Deal?

There are many different kinds of poker games. We will deal, however, with the card games played in the states mentioned.

In California, for example, only closed poker is allowed, i.e., draw poker, five cards, jacks or better, and five card lowball. The state of California, for some reason, does not allow stud poker—only draw or lowball poker. Stud poker is the game in which one gets two or three cards dealt face down, then four cards dealt up, for a six or seven card game. Five card stud is where four cards are dealt up with one card down (in the hole). Then there is the popular game of seven card stud, where there are four cards open and three down cards in your hand. There's also high-low draw, and high-low stud, which gives a win to both the high hand and the low hand. Then there is the variation, played mostly in tournaments, called Hold'em, which we will explain in detail. Lowball is a game in which the lowest hand wins. A straight of ace-2-3-4-5 is the lowest hand. Ace counts for one, and the second lowest hand is ace-2-3-4-6, then ace-2-3-5-6, and so on.

These are the most popular games played in the various card rooms and poker clubs around the country. Now here are explanations of each game, starting with draw poker.

Draw Poker

The first requirement of the game is to *ante*, which means that a previously agreed-upon amount of money is placed on the table by each player. This serves the dual purpose of giving each player an incentive to win and at the same time helps to eliminate the problem of the proverbial quitter who always folds unless he instantly draws four to a royal flush.

Next, five cards are dealt face down to each player and it is time to determine who is going to open the betting and then who is going to *call* (match the bet) or raise it. The general rule is that it takes a pair of jacks or better to open. This is when you have to exercise caution and have the necessary knowledge to make an accurate analysis of the odds. The odds depend upon how many players are involved, where you are sitting, and who opens before you. Speaking in very general terms, the odds are quite high that everyone is going to be dealt at least one pair. If you happen to have a pair of jacks, the probability that someone else has a pair of queens or kings is very high. Out of the heart of Texas comes a quote that is extremely appropriate here: "I don't open with jacks. That's gambling and my Daddy taught me never to gamble."

Pay close attention to the odds. It would be an excellent idea to pick up one of the many available books on analyzing the odds and study it until you can commit most of it to memory. If you are capable of accurately understanding the odds, you will be way ahead of the opponent who goes on hunches and gut-level feelings. Their "feelings" will probably end up putting money in your pockets.

The easiest rule of thumb would be that if you are sitting directly to the left of the deal, then open with aces. If you are two seats or more from the dealer, open with nothing lower than kings. If someone in the seventh seat opens first, figure that they have at least a pair of jacks, and don't stay in the game unless you have at least a pair of queens. If you plan to raise the opening bet, then be sure that you can beat any pair. The rules on betting vary from game to game and go all the way from unlimited betting to the more common system of having a fixed amount and/or a fixed number of raises.

Now all the betting for this round has come to a halt and you are ready to draw. Again there are variations on the theme. You can "rebuild" your hand by discarding from one to five cards (the latter amount only if allowed) and getting new ones in exchange. If you have a *pat* hand, you are satisfied with the original cards dealt to you in the first place. Again there are odds to consider and, as mentioned earlier, if there is $10 in the pot and you are betting $2, then your return, if you win, will be 5 to 1. What you must consider is that if your cards indicate that the odds are 22 to 1 that you won't win, then you should not be staying in the game because the odds of winning should be better than the pot odds.

Once you know your odds and, based on the laws of probability, it appears that you have the winning hand, go for it, all the way! If you're running scared about losing your shirt, you shouldn't be in the game in the first place. Part of the battle is to come to the table armed with the proper knowledge; the other part is to back yourself up financially, without a doubt, once you're ready to make your move.

One final note: It's best not to play poker with people you've never met before. It's hard enough to "read" the expressions of people you know, let alone to come out ahead with a bunch of total strangers.

Five Card Stud

Unlike draw poker, there is only one hidden card in this game—the first one, which is dealt face down. Before the betting, one more card is dealt face up. Then after each round of betting, another card is dealt until you have five.

In this game, the main thing to look for is a pair of *anything*. A pair of twos can easily take you straight to the bank because of the limited amount of cards dealt in this game.

One of the ways to psych out your opponents is to notice if anyone keeps checking his down card. It couldn't be all that great if he can't even remember what it is!

Now, if you're hoping to pick up the fourth and or fifth card to a straight or a flush, you are treading in deep water. The only time you would stay in under these circumstances would be if no one is betting, in which case you can *check*, meaning you get a free ride this time around. In this game, if you're being stared in the face by an ace in someone else's hand, look around for other aces. If one or two others are exposed also, the chances are slim to none that anyone will get their pair.

If you've definitely got the only game in town, play somewhat cautiously. You don't want to scare everyone off by your overly bold betting. Keep everyone interested, if you can, and then grab the money and run.

Seven Card Stud

Two more cards and what do you get? Seven card stud, a most interesting game that is full of unexpected variables. Part of the intrigue is that the first two cards and the last card are dealt face down and the other four are exposed. Also, the pot gets bigger because there is an extra round of betting.

With two cards down, it is a lot more difficult to figure out what's going on in your opponents' hands. Also, there are many schools of thought on how to play this game. Some people arbitrarily stay in to get their fourth card before they decide whether to fold or not. A lot of good players stay in only if they have a pair concealed or perhaps a split pair and, of course, anything better.

The best clue to look for is this: If you are beaten on sight after four cards are dealt, it is a good time to fold your hand. Please be forewarned, though, that to stay in on a hunch or a hope is usually a losing proposition.

One rule of thumb is to pay close attention to the big bettors who *appear* to have "nothing much" going for them. It's very easy to get deceived in this game, so if you don't have the cards to play and you stay. . . you'll pay!

High/Low Draw

If you already know how to play draw poker, then the only change now is that the pot will be split between the high and low hands. The amateur player has a tendency to shy away from going for a high hand. Holding out for a low hand can be terribly disappointing when a one-eyed jack is staring you right in the face, especially after you have just bet your life savings during the last three betting rounds. There are two major variations: one where the players declare whether they are going for high or low or both, the other where "cards speak."

High/Low Seven Card Stud

This game has an interesting twist. . . you can go either high or low and, in some cases, both high and low. Since you have seven cards to rearrange any way you want, you can often set up a good low hand and then find out you have the winning high straight as well. According to one set of rules, if you are going both high and low (often known as going *pig*) and someone else has you beat for either high or low, you are completely out of the game.

Hold'em

The rules are a bit unusual because it's a seven card stud game, but you share five common cards in the middle of the table with the other players. So, with the exception of the first two cards dealt down to you, everyone has what everyone else has. Depending on how you look at it, this can be one of the most exciting or most anxiety-producing games in town. As in seven card stud, you are still looking for the best five cards. There's just enough intrigue to keep everyone on the edge of their seats. This game definitely could be subtitled "Bluffer's Paradise." The betting occurs first after each player is dealt his two hole cards; then after the first three community cards (called the *flop*) are turned over; then when each of the last two cards are individually turned (called *fourth* and *fifth street*, respectively).

Lowball

As the name implies, it is the lowest hand that wins this game. However, the rules vary on how to arrive at the winning hand. According to one set of official rules, aces are low; so therefore, a pair of aces is lower than a pair of deuces. Also, straights don't count, so the perfect low would be ace through five (often referred to as a *bicycle*). On the other hand, there is another way to play it with straights being high and, therefore, the perfect low would be ace, 2, 3, 4, and 6. . . and still a third way, called *Razz*, where the ace is high, as are straights and flushes, and the lowest hand is 2, 3, 4, 5, 7.

Poker Terminology

ANTE—To place an agreed-upon amount of money on the table before the draw. Each player bets the same amount.

BLUFF—The ability to misrepresent one's hand.

CALL—To match the previous bet.

CHECK—When the player passes on his turn.

DRAW—The basic style of poker in which each player is dealt five cards, face down, jacks or better to open.

FIVE-CARD STUD—The type of poker in which only the first card is dealt face down, and the other four are face up.

FLUSH—Any five cards, all of the same suit.

FOLD—What a player does when he tosses his cards face down, thus eliminating himself from that hand. When he folds, the player forfeits any ante or previous bets.

FOUR OF A KIND—Any four cards of the same denomination, i.e., four queens, four 9s, etc.

FULL HOUSE—A hand with three of a kind and two of a kind, of any denomination.

HIGH-LOW DRAW—Draw poker, in which the pot is split between the highest and lowest hands.

HIGH-LOW STUD—A version of poker played with seven cards, in which each player can wager an arrangement of cards as being either the highest or lowest—or playing both (called *playing pig*) a high and low arrangement.

HOLD 'EM—A variation of seven-card poker in which five common cards are shared by the players, and two cards more are held by each player individually.

JOKER—A card used as a *wild card*. In California poker clubs, the joker may be used for aces, straights and flushes only.

LOWBALL—A version of poker in which the low hand wins.

PAIR—Two of a kind.

PASS—To *not* bet.

POT—The total number of chips bet in the hand from the first bet to the final bet.

RAISE—To increase the previous bet.

ROYAL FLUSH—The 10, jack, queen, king and ace of one suit. This is poker's top hand.

SEVEN-CARD STUD—Seven-card poker, in which the first two and last card are dealt face down, and the other four are exposed.

STRAIGHT FLUSH—Five cards of the same suit in sequence.

TRIPS—Three of a kind.

WILD CARD—A card which can be used in place of any other card in the deck. This card is predetermined by house rules.

Chapter 8
Backgammon: The Basics...
and a Little More

Backgammon, one of mankind's most dearly-regarded games, has been popular for centuries. Its fascination is based on the fact that the game is actually a combination of skill and luck, with plenty of opportunity for the player with savvy to turn any roll of the dice to his advantage.

This chapter will discuss the fundamental rules of the game of backgammon, as well as the various strategies of play that can be chosen as the game develops. You will learn the meaning of the *running* game and the *back* game, and how to accomplish them. *Blots, blocks* and *builders* will also be discussed.

A Look at the Board

Backgammon is played by two people seated opposite each other at either side of a board which is divided into four sections, or *quarters*. Each quarter has six long, pointed triangles, called *points*, which each represent a numerical place on the board. Each player has 15 *stones*, or small playing discs, that are usually black for one player and white for another. In some fancy backgammon sets, the colors can be red and white, or green and white, but the toned pieces are referred to as "black" for convenience.

The player's inner table will be the quarter in which he must aim to assemble all his stones so that he can begin *bearing them off*, or moving them off the playing board. The player moves his stones from the opponent's inner table through the opponent's outer table, then into his own outer table and, finally, to his inner table. Only after all of his stones are present back in his inner table can he begin to bear off his stones. As seen in Diagram 8-1, White's inner table is on his left while his outer table is on his right; for Black, it is vice versa.

Take a moment now to study Diagram 8-1 and look at the numbered points, seeing the direction in which each player's stones will have to move in order to get ahead of his opponent.

Diagram 8-1

Getting Started

The next question is, how are the backgammon moves made? The players take turns rolling two dice in a dice cup. The dice are the usual kind with numbers one to six represented on each cube. Keep in mind that the two numbers coming up on the dice (for example, a 4 and 2 to make a total of 6) must be viewed and responded to one at a time, even if the player ends up moving four steps and two steps with the same stone. He can, of course, move one stone four and another two, but cannot break up the steps any other way (such as five and one or three and three). The dice must be obeyed exactly!

At the start of the game, the stones are arranged as follows: Two stones are placed on the opponent's 1-point, five on the opponent's 12-point, three on the player's own 8-point and five on his 6-point. The player's first objective is to get all of his stones *home* to his inner table; his next objective is to bear off all his stones before his opponent, and thus win the game.

A couple of rules must be kept in mind for moving the stones. One is that the stones never change direction; they cannot move backward. Also, when choosing which stone to move with the dice, it must be remembered that no player can place a stone on a point occupied by two or more of his opponent's stones. If, on the other hand, a player's throw of the dice causes him to move a stone to a point where just one of his opponent's stones is resting, he can knock out that stone and send it back *to the bar* (the center divider between the inner and outer tables), where it must wait for a suitable roll to be reentered to the game. Such a single stone is called a *blot*. Two or more of the opponent's stones on a point is referred to as a *block*.

A player always uses his full throw (that is, the numbers on both dice) to move whenever possible. Toward the climax of the game, when more and more of the points might contain blocks for him and he finds it impossible to utilize the entire roll, he uses the large number if possible. Barring that, he will use the smaller dice if he must. But if he finds there is no way for him to use either number on the dice to make a move, he forfeits his turn to his opponent.

A double number rolled on the dice is fortunate, because it also doubles the player's roll. In other words, a 4 and 4 thrown actually become 4 and 4 and 4 and 4, which can be used on anywhere from one to four different stones to advance them. On doubles, two stones can be moved together, if desired, establishing a new block for the player on a fresh point.

Needless to say, it is strategic to attempt to move a stone onto a point where one or more of your own stones already are. To move a lone stone onto a new point deems it a blot, and vulnerable to attack by your rival. As in many other things, when it comes to moving your stones, there's safety in numbers.

Also remember that when a blot of yours is hit and sent to the bar by your rival, you must use your next roll to reenter that stone. If, because of blocks, you cannot reenter your blot with the numbers you've rolled, then you are stymied; you can't move until such time as you can come up with a roll that makes this possible. So, avoid unprotected stones!

As always, there's an exception to this rule. In some cases, strategic players will take a calculated risk on a blot, because for them it is the first step in establishing a block; in other words, the first lone stone is a *builder* that will later be joined by another stone, if possible, on the following roll. But this is always a risky maneuver and the odds should be weighed carefully before proceeding with it.

Things to Remember

The *priorities* of backgammon should always be kept in the player's mind. First priority: Getting all stones into the inner table. Next priority: Bearing them off. But also important are: forming blocks to stymie your opponent's progress, hitting blots to send to the bar, and avoiding blots yourself. Every roll of the dice should be used to implement these objectives, preferably more than one objective at a time.

If a player manages to bear off all his stones before his opponent, he wins the game. But a double win is provided if he can manage this feat before his player has borne off even one stone. Then the win is called a *gammon*. Even better than a gammon is a *backgammon*, in which a player accomplishes the bearing off of all his stones while the opponent still has one or more stones in the winner's inner table, or at the bar. This type of win is equivalent to winning three games!

There are a couple of rules to remember about bearing off. As mentioned before, no stone can be borne off until all the player's stones are present in his own inner table. Also, an exact roll is needed to move the stone off the board. In other words, if Black has a stone on his own 4-point, only a roll of 4 would permit its exit from the board. On a six, a die with 6 is needed, or a 4 and 2, to exit the stone, and so forth.

At each roll of the dice, the player should mentally run through all possible moves made available by the roll, and try to go for the one that will serve the most different objectives. Merely advancing a stone forward is not enough. The player should advance forward into a block, move another piece to hit the opponent's blot, or set up a *prime* (six blocks adjacently held); in this way, accomplishing not only his own progress, but the hindrance of the advancement of his opponent.

Whether one plays a *blocking game* (in which one concentrates mainly on blocking the opponent's progress toward bearing off), or a *running game* (in which the main objective is rushing to bear off one's own stones), depends heavily on how the game shapes up after the first few rolls. Backgammon is one game in which the player who starts the game (determined by the initial roll) has a heavy advantage. At the start of the game, each player rolls a single dice, and the one with the higher number starts the game. His starting roll is the combination of his number and his opponent's. If they tie, they must roll again, until one of the players has a higher figure. This one starting roll can give a player a clear edge that is difficult to cancel out.

Let's Play

Let's say White gets to go first and rolls a wonderful 6-5, which allows him to advance from 1B to 7B, and from 12B to 8W. Then Black rolls a 6-4. This allows him to, if he wishes, move one of his *runners*, or black stones, from 1W to 7W, so building his *bar point*; but isn't it more strategic, in terms of the aims mentioned above, to use his 6 to go from 12W to 7B, hitting White's blot and sending it to the bar, and take his 4 as a move from 12B to 9B, where White would need a total of 8 to hurt it? This isn't all that likely, so it would be a safe move. All Black would have to worry about, in this instance, is the possibility that White would roll a 7 or 8 combination, hitting one of these two temporary blots. Provided this doesn't happen, Black could use his next turn to double up on those blots.

The above example is, admittedly, a risky one, because it does leave Black with two blots, on 7B and 8B, for the time being. But it is always better to combine an advancing move with a *hit* of your opponent's blot, than to merely make an innocuous move that does you some good but does your opponent no harm.

On his next roll, White gets a 5 and 4. He can use the 5 to reenter from the bar, and make his 5-point by joining this stone with the one left on 1B. This powerful block is an effective retaliation for your hit.

Always remember the principle of combining your own advancement with your opponent's effective deterrent. Then you will be on your way to winning backgammon.

Playing Options

Sometimes, if you have a series of low rolls working against you, and your opponent seems to be zipping ahead with several high numbers in a row, you might consider adopting a *back game* strategy. The back game, or defensive-type game, is one in which you concentrate mainly on forming blocks in strategic places to deter your opponent's progress, and hitting as many of his blots as possible to stymie him.

By using four and six back men to make two or three points in your opponent's inner table, effectively blocking his bearing off, you are spoiling many of his rolls; by sending his blots to the bar, you can effectively clear the way for some of your runners to make it into your own inner table. As one well known backgammon connoisseur, Professor Hoffmann, points out, no one should begin a game of backgammon with the intent of playing a back game, but any player must be prepared to deal with the necessity of playing one should it arise.

The bearing-off stage of backgammon, where all the strategy

begins to pay off, can be very tricky. One must play a smart game when bringing one's stones into the inner table by not crowding them all on one or two low numbers; this quickly makes the odds against bearing them off impossibly high. Remember to keep a well-distributed board, with all (or most) points of the inner table effectively covered. This will ensure that a wide range of numbers coming up on the dice can be used to bear off, rather than just one or two low numbers which can be difficult to throw.

Acey-Deucy

You've just read a summary of rules and tips for basic backgammon. There is, however, a form of the game known as *acey-deucy*. This originated in America during World War II, and is being rediscovered of late. In acey-deucy, the same routes for black and white stones are followed, with the exception that there is no opening arrangement of stones on the board; the game begins with all four tables clear, and the players enter their stones onto the board according to the roll of the dice, with no restrictions for entering and moving. If a player rolls a 1–2, it is called an *acey-deucy*, and entitles him not only to that number of moves, but also gives him the privilege of chosing any double roll he wishes, laying it down, and moving his stones accordingly. Additionally, he is given an extra roll of the dice before his turn is through.

As an example, if Black starts the game by rolling a 1–2, he can open with one man on 1W and another on 2W. He could then choose double-six to play, putting an additional two men on 6W and then moving them to 12W. Then, on his second roll, if he came up with 4–3, he could move a man from 1W to 5W and another from 2W to 5W, making a block.

Of course, in the beginning stages of the game, the 1–2 roller would do well to maximize his luck by choosing a double-six for maximum progress. As the game goes on, however, and blocks abound, he may be forced to go with a lower double, else forfeit not only this shot but his bonus roll as well.

A good strategy in acey-deucy would be to get half your men

together on the board as soon as possible, since you have no ready-made blocks to begin with the way you do in regular backgammon. A player in this version of the game should try to form blocks with his runners as early in the game as he can.

An important difference between acey-deucy and regular backgammon is that whereas in regular backgammon, a blot that is hit must be reentered before any other men can be moved, the same is not true of acey-deucy. In the latter version, a man that is *hit* can be reentered at any time.

Chouette

Another version of backgammon, called *chouette*, involves one player, called the *man in the box*, pitted against a team. This player is determined by the high roller of the dice. The second-highest roller becomes the captain of the team, and makes all the movement decisions for his team, after consulting the other players. If the man in the box wins, he collects from the other team and stays *in the box* for another game, and the captain goes to the bottom of the team, with the other players moving up a place and a new captain taking over. If the man in the box loses, he pays off each player and goes to the foot of the team, while the captain becomes the man in the box and the players move up, with the previous second-ranking player taking over.

The Doubling Cube

When playing a *doubling game* (in which the stakes are doubled), serious players keep track of how the doubling stands by using a *doubling cube*—a special cube which has the numbers 2,4,8,16,32 and 64 engraved on different sides. Whoever makes the first double brings the cube to his end of the table and lays it with the 2 side upward. If his opponent later redoubles, it goes to the opponent's end and he turns the 4 side upward. This continues as long as redoubles are proposed and accepted. If declined, the final doubler wins and collects.

Backgammon Terminology

ACE-POINT—Another word for the 1-point position.

ACEY-DEUCY—A roll of 1–2 on the dice. It also refers to a form of backgammon in which this roll gives the player a choice of doubles and another roll.

AUTOMATIC DOUBLE—This is a rule which when implemented doubles the stakes if each player rolls the same number (i.e., making a double roll) at the beginning of the game.

BACK GAME—This is one in which a player might purposely set up blots, which are hit and sent to the bar, so he can reenter them to form blocks in his opponent's inner table.

BACKGAMMON—A game in which the winner scores three times the value of a single game by bearing off all of his stones before his opponent bears off even one, and while there is still one of his rival's stones on the winner's inner table or the bar.

BACK MAN—A stone on the opponent's inner table. The game opens with two *back men* on the opponent's 1-point; back men are also any stones reentered from the bar.

BACKWARD GAME—This is the act of keeping *back men* in your opponent's inner table to prevent him from bearing off, thus paralyzing his game. This technique is useful in offsetting a losing game.

BAR—The divider where stones are sent (blots) when they are hit. The bar runs lengthwise between the inner and outer tables.

BAR POINT—A player's 7-point location, the first point in his outer table.

BEARING OFF—Moving stones from one's own inner table off the board; the last stage in winning the game. Bearing off can only be done when all the player's stones are home in his own inner table, and then only on exact rolls for exit.

BLOCK—Two or more stones placed on a single point, which prohibits the opponent's stones from landing there.

BLOCKING GAME—A game in which the focus is on forming a series of blocks to impede the other player's advance.

BLOT—A single stone on one point. It is vulnerable because it can be hit by the rival's stone and sent to the bar, stopping the player's game until he can reenter it.

BOARD—The backgammon playing board; also can be used instead of table, as in *inner board* for *inner table,* etc.

BONUS ROLL—Another roll of the dice granted to a player who rolls a 1–2 in the version of the game known as acey-deucy.

BOX—As in *man in the box,* the position of the one player who takes on the entire team in the chouette version of backgammon.

BUILDER—A blot or extra stone, placed in a position where it *makes a point* or helps establish a block.

CAPTAIN—The head of a team of players in chouette who play the *man in the box.*

CATCHERS—Stones that a player has distributed throughout his board to, he hopes, catch his rival's runners and send them to the bar. This technique is often used in back games.

CHOUETTE—In this type of backgammon, a lone player, or *man in the box,* takes on an entire team of opposition, headed by a captain.

COMFORT STATION—A nickname for the opponent's 12-point. It is thus named because the player, having started the game with this point made, can stop his runners off there on the way to his own side of the board.

COVERING—The act of making a point occupied by a blot, by moving another stone to that point, thus covering the blot.

CUP—Short for dice cup.

DICE—Two cubes, with the six sides of each numbered from one to six with dots, which are rolled or thrown to determine the number of moves one makes on the board.

DICE CUP—A special cup from which the dice are rolled in backgammon.

DOUBLE—To increase the stakes in backgammon to double the original amount.

DOUBLE GAME—Another term for a *gammon*.

DOUBLES—A roll of the dice in which both dice come up with the same number, as in 3-3. Doubles give the player twice as much point value to move as is shown.

DOUBLING CUBE—A special cube—usually marked with 2, 4, 8, 16, 32, 64—which players use alternately to double the stakes.

DOUBLING GAME—A modern version of the game in which a player may, according to the regulations, double the stakes during the course of play.

ENTER—To bring in a stone from the bar to the opponent's home board

FORWARD GAME—A favorable game, or *aggressive* game, in which a player uses his favorable rolls to move stones quickly without taking unnecessary risks.

GAME—To bear off all stones before your opponent can do the same.

GAMMON—A game in which the winner scores twice the value of one game by bearing off all his stones before his opponent can bear off even one.

HIT—To move a stone to a point occupied by your opponent's blot and send it to the bar. A win of regular backgammon is sometimes called a *hit* as well.

HOME BOARD—Sometimes the player's inner table is referred to by this term.

HOYLE COUNT—The traditional way of determining which player has the lead. The player counts any stone on his 1-point as having a value of one; on his 2-point, a value of two; and so forth up to his 6-point. Then he counts how many points are needed to bring all of his stones to his 6-point. He then calculates his opponent's stones in the same way; the one with the smaller total is the leading player.

IDEAL ROLL—A 6–1 combination on an opening throw; some say 3–1 is also ideal.

INNER TABLE—The section of the backgammon board that includes points 1 to 6. This is divided into Black's inner table and White's inner table.

IN THE BOX—A term used in chouette, as in *man in the box*, to describe the player who is opposing the entire team.

KEY POINTS—Points preferred to be made as soon as possible in the game, usually the player's own 5-point, or his opponent's 5-point; followed by the bar point (7-point), and a player's own 4-point.

KNOCK OFF—To hit the opponent's block and send it to the bar. This term is used in acey-deucy.

LOVER'S LEAP—An opening or early move from the opponent's 1-point to his 12-point, as a result of a lucky 6–5 roll of the dice.

MAKE A POINT—To place two or more stones on a point, thus creating an effective block to your opponent.

MEN—Stones.

ODDS—The various chances involving hits, bearing off, and other possibilities of the game; also the probabilities of various rolls of the dice.

OUTER TABLE—The section of the board from points 7 to 12. This is subdivided into Black's outer table and White's outer table.

PLAYING SAFE—Moving stones to points already made by your other stones, rather than letting them sit alone as blots.

POINT—Any of the 24 long triangles on which the stones sit on their way to bearing off. The term also applies to a triangle that has been *made* by placing two or more stones on it so the opponent cannot land there.

POINT COUNT—See Hoyle's Count.

PRIME—Six adjacent points made with blocks and held by one player, forming a barrier his opponent can't pass.

RAIL—Another term for the bar.

REENTERING—Bringing stones back from the bar.

RUNNER—A back man which a player hopes to bring from his rival's inner table by running it past any blocks the rival may have set up.

RUNNING GAME—Similar to a forward game. It becomes a full-fledged running game when a player gets all his stones past his opponent's blocks, running them all to his own inner table and bearing them off quickly.

SPLITTING RUNNERS—To move one runner ahead of its companion.

STONE—One of 15 playing pieces, or discs, used in backgammon.

TABLE—A section of the backgammon board.

TAKING OFF—Same as bearing off.

THROW—A roll of the dice, especially when using the dice cup.

THROW OFF—To bear off or take off.

TRIC TRAC or TRICK TRACK—Old name for backgammon.

TRIPLE GAME—A backgammon win in which one has borne off all his stones while his opponent still has not borne off any, and still has stones in his own (the winner's) inner table, or at the bar.

WALKING A PRIME—To move a prime of six blocks along the board by moving stones from the back toward the front to replace others that have moved forward. A very effective method of play when it can be accomplished.

Chapter 9
Gin Rummy:
How to Play
Gin and Win

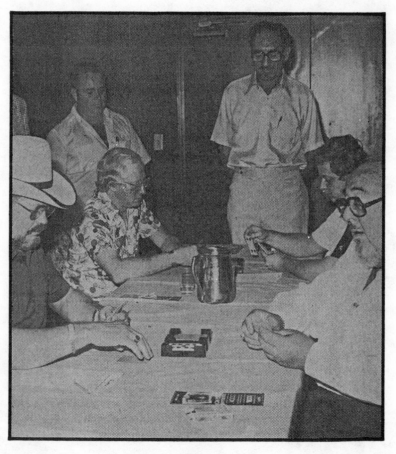

An Introduction to the Game

It would be easy to presume that gin rummy is merely a game of luck. After all, only the Fates decide what kind of a hand you get, right? But that's not the whole story. Obviously, if you have a ragtag hand of unmatchables and your opponent's is studded with aces and lined-up royalty. . . the odds are naturally against your walking away with the pot. But by being a clever player, you can maximize whatever assets you have, keep a sharp eye on the discard pile, and cut your losses to a minimum.

Gin rummy is played with an ordinary 52-card deck. The king is the highest card, the ace is the lowest. Picture cards count 10; all other cards count their numerical face value, including the ace which is 1. The deck is cut, and the player with the low card deals. The players are dealt 10 cards apiece alternately (two players at a time), and the twenty-first card is turned up and placed next to the remainder of the deck. The first player has the option of adding this exposed card to his hand and discarding one; or turning over a new card from the deck, keeping that and discarding one card; or discarding the new card and keeping his hand as is. The players continue in this manner until one player has gin and exposes his hand, or a player announces he is *knocking*, or exiting, the game with an unmelded value of 10 or less.

The mechanics of *melding* are widely known but worth reviewing. Three of a kind, or three or more sequential cards of the same suit, constitute *meld* possibilities. An entirely *melded* hand is *gin* and terminates the round. The game continues until one player reaches a total score of 100 points (in some locales, gin rummy is played until a winning score of 500 is reached).

Knowing the Score

The scoring in gin rummy works as follows. The *knocker*, or the first player to exit the game with an *unmelded* total of 10 or under, collects the points totaled from the unmelded cards of his opponent. This is called a *box* or *line* score. Keep in mind that the player who *knocks* only wins the box score if his unmelded count is less than that of his opponent. If he knocks with a value of say, 8, and his opponent's unmelded value is only 6, the opponent wins the box score, which in this case will be the difference between the knocker's and his own (in this case, 2) plus a 25-point bonus. If the opponent and the knocker tie in their unmelded values, the opponent wins the hand, scoring 25 points.

Before the score is totaled, the opponent of the knocker may add any of his own unmelded cards to the knocker's melds, if he can, thus cancelling out those points. Unmatched cards equal to the knocking count (usually 10) are also discarded. The remainder of his cards are added to the knocker's score.

In the event of *gin*, the winner collects the points of his opponent's unmelded cards, none of which may be added to his melds. That and a 25-point bonus constitutes his score for the hand.

When the game is over, the final scoring is tallied by giving each player an additional 10 points for each box, and giving the winner the difference in points between his score and his opponent's. Additionally, the winner receives 100 extra points for winning the game. In the case of a *schneider*—a player who reaches 100 points without permitting his opponent to score at all—the winner receives double-point value for everything, including box scores and the game bonus.

(In the version called "Oklahoma Gin," the knocking value is determined by the value of the twenty-first card turned up. If the card is an ace, there is no knocking and the game is for *gin*.)

The Best Strategy For Winning

Most players of gin rummy automatically assume that they should play for *gin*, as this is the way to win big. But, looking at it from a purely mathematical standpoint, *gin* is the long-shot of the game and you'd be better off playing to knock!

Rather than holding on to high cards in the hopes that you will be able to meld them and achieve *gin*, you're much better off reducing the numerical count of your hand as quickly as possible so that you can knock. The deck should be viewed—as well as your hand—as to its *knocking* possibilities for you, not its *gin* possibilities. Remember to knock as soon as you can, because it's dollars to doughnuts that if you don't, your opponent will!

Be very careful with the cards you throw off. If you have even an inkling that your opponent needs a certain card, by all means keep it and readjust your strategy accordingly. *NEVER* throw out a card your opponent can use: this is the sure way to be a loser at gin rummy.

The discard pile is very important—watch it carefully. With a little good sense, the discard pile will map out for you your opponent's *gin* strategy and help you determine how to play your own hand.

When analyzing your hand, remember to always give more credence to the low cards, as they will do you far more good than the high ones. Don't hold on to high pairs hoping for a meld which may never happen, and don't pass up card after card with a value of four or under. This will get you nowhere. Your opponent may very well knock or *gin* first, and you will be sunk to the tune of those high unmelded cards! Cards with a value of six or more, therefore, should only be picked up when they *immediately* make you a meld. Otherwise, forget it—they're too much of a risk in the long run.

Playing Wisely

In terms of concealing your own strategy from your opponent, it is obviously preferable to choose the card from the deck (which your opponent has not seen) than to pick up the one he has just discarded. Even if you have a very poor hand, you're getting desperate, and the latest cast-off will make you a pair, look at it this way: A pair is still not a meld, and if you hold a slew of unmatched cards, the hidden card may provide you with a pair as well, without letting your opponent know where you're at. Even if it doesn't, it could be a low card which will help you knock faster. Only open cards which will form immediate melds (*not* meld possibilities, such as pairs) should be picked up.

Keep in mind that your goal is to knock as quickly as possible. Therefore, a high card or an open card which will allow you to knock immediately upon your discard should, of course, be picked up! There are exceptions to every rule.

Watch the open cards, and when your opponent picks one up, do your best to discern his strategy. If, for example, you've noticed a 7 of diamonds in the discard pile, you've got the 9 of diamonds, and your opponent takes the 8 of diamonds when it comes up, it's a cinch he's melding 8s. But what if the other player picks up the 4 of clubs when you've got the 3 of clubs and the 4 of hearts? He could be melding 4s or 4-5-6-ing it. In this case, you'd better hold on to both cards—no real hardship in this instance because they are low cards. Even if the value were high, however, it would be preferable to hold on to them, despite their knocking risk, than to throw out one of them and take the greater, more punitive risk of handing your opponent the game.

*   *   *

Always think this way about discards—not just in terms of what the discard will do for your own hand, but in terms of what it *could* do for your opponent's. Once you're sure your opponent needs a card for a meld, it is imperative that you keep this card even if said card puts you in a temporary deadlock. There are ways around the deadlock by slightly altering your strategy... but there's no way around handing your opponent another meld! Even if the card is a total "foreigner" to your own hand and doesn't fit in anywhere, it pays to sacrifice a pair—even a low pair—to keep it. In fact, if the number value hasn't yet been played (or consecutives) and you don't need it, the chances are more than good your opponent does! Or else why hasn't it appeared before?

This is particularly true when you are well into the game. Don't feel too badly about keeping a *non-ginning* card; you may be able to throw it off later when your opponent is well into another tack. Or you can discard it when you knock; or if your opponent knocks first, you might be able to lay it off on a meld of his.

Always try to knock early in the game: this will greatly increase your chances of catching your opponent with many high, unmatched cards to add to your score. If you can't knock by the tenth card or so, it's time to play for *gin*. This is because well into the game, your opponent has a good chance of knowing pretty much what your melds are, especially if you've picked a lot of open cards. He could probably lay off a lot of unmatched cards on your melds should you decide to knock. So even if *gin* is a long-shot for you toward the end of the game, it's better to wait for *him* to knock, and use lay-offs for self-defense, getting your knocking count below his.

Once you decide to play for *gin*, remember not to make two four-card melds. Pairs don't work, so that will force you to complete two melds to *gin* instead of just one. If, for example, you hold a 10-J-Q-K of clubs, an 8 of clubs, 8 of hearts and 8 of spades, a pair of 3s, and a 4, it would be silly to pick up an 8 of diamonds and discard the 4 if one of the 3s and the 4 were the same suit. You don't need the 8 of diamonds, and by holding on to the 4 you double your chances of achieving *gin*.

Make A Note...

To summarize, try to remember these points in the game of gin rummy:

(1) Your first priority should be to *knock*, not hold out for *gin*.
(2) Knock early in the game.
(3) Favor low cards over high ones, in general.
(4) Do your best to keep cards your opponent needs.
(5) Pick up only those high cards that will immediately meld.
(6) Pay attention to the discard pile; watch it constantly.
(7) Pick only open cards that immediately *meld*, not merely *pair*.

(8) Always try to keep both cards when you're not sure which one will help the other player.

(9) If you can't knock by the tenth discard, play for *gin*.

(10) Avoid making two four-card melds.

Follow these rules, and you will be well on your way to establishing a reputation as the "gin whiz" of your set.

Gin Rummy Terminology

BOX SCORE—The points a player makes by knocking and receiving the point value of all of his opponent's unmelded cards.

GIN—The way to win the game of gin rummy: having all 10 cards melded.

KNOCK, KNOCKING—The way a player can score the round by getting his unmelded cards' point value down to 10 or under; in this way, he gains the points of his opponent's unmelded cards.

LINE SCORE—The same as the *box score*.

MELD—To combine three or more cards either of the same denomination or same suit in sequence. A group of three or more such cards.

OKLAHOMA GIN—In this variation of the game, the knocking card—or the one whose value determines the point value under which a player must bring his unmelded cards in order to knock—is the first card of the deck turned up. If an ace is turned up, there is no knocking and the game is strictly for gin.

SCHNEIDER—What is achieved when a player reaches a total score of 100 points—whether by knocking or ginning—before his opponent can score even once. This feat doubles his score.

Chapter 10
Money Management:
A Method for Winning More and Losing Less

Money management is definitely an integral part of casino gaming. Whichever table games you're playing (craps, blackjack, baccarat, roulette), it is necessary to do two things: limit your losses and magnify your wins. This objective can be accomplished through proper money management. It's a simple thing to come by, and in this chapter we're going to tell you about money management and how it can help you to win more money and limit your losses, giving you a much nicer vacation wherever you may go for gaming fun and excitement.

Self-Control is the Key

To start with, the term "money management" has to do with the control of your bets so that, on one hand, you reduce the loss risk to a stipulated amount, but on the winning side, there are no restrictions. Yes, it's the perfect method of betting. It can account for winning more money when your luck is good, when the dice are rolling well, when blackjack is hitting. . .whatever the game may be. On the other hand, when you're not winning, you will learn through money management how to conserve your bankroll.

Money management, in a word, is a form of *discipline*. Your money management starts to work almost immediately upon arriving at your gaming site. As soon as you walk into the hotel, it's a matter of not rushing to put a dollar in a slot machine, $5 on the craps table, $1 on the spin of a roulette wheel. . .or whatever the amount, or whatever the game. The idea in money management is that you *plan* your forays into the various table games. All of this, incidentally, simply adds to the pleasure, the fun, and the excitement at your favorite game, as well as your winning potential. So, tne first thing you do upon checking into the hotel is to divide your bankroll into certain amounts. For example, let's say that you are there for a two-day stay, and during your stay you're obviously going to play at the tables, dine, see some shows, and enjoy various forms of entertainment. The difference between winning and losing money is sometimes definitely affected by how well you're enjoying your holiday.

A Betting Exercise

Let's say you're playing with $400 over a period of two days. You're going to divide that $400 into four sessions on one day and four sessions on another day. Four hundred is divided into eight equal parts to start; if you win money, things can change, as you will see. So you wind up with $50 per session. A session means you take that $50, walk over to the craps (or roulette, etc.) table, and that is the money you're going to gamble with during that playing session. The playing session ends when you walk away from the table, having lost that $50. If, on the other hand, you walk away with chips to cash in, that also ends that playing session.

Now you go to the table, hand the dealer $50 at a $5 minimum table, and get 10 $5 chips back for our cash money. If you refer back to our section on how to play winning craps, you'll know how to do what we suggested. But let's say you put $5 on the line, the shooter rolls a point, and you play $5 back on the line because you want to get your full odds, and after a few rolls you've lost $10. Well, the next shooter comes up and, in many cases, people will start to double up at this point, figuring, "Well, I lost the last time, so I'm gonna try ten dollars this time, and see if I can recoup my lost money." Well, that's wrong. In money management, and this is one of the strictest rules, you never double up on a previous loss. You do not increase your bet in any way on a previous loss.

So, according to our procedure, you place another $5 bet, and if again the shooter rolls a 4, you've got $5 in back of the line. Remember, when you're betting the line, you always take the odds in back, because that brings the percentage way down. Your *pass line* bets always pay even money. Your *odds* bets, which can be the equivalent of the amount of money on the *pass line*, can give you higher odds and bigger winnings.

Lo and behold, let's say the shooter rolls another 7 and you've lost. You're now $20 out. Again, you are faced with the temptation of doubling up to win. But that's not how it works. There's no such thing as hunches, lucky feelings, etc.; they just don't work at the craps table.

Again, after your second loss, you put $5 on the line. Now the shooter rolls, up comes a 7, and you win $5. This is your first win, and according to our procedure, we always double the amount of the bet on our first win. So this time, after the dealer pays you $5, you double up and $10 go on the line. The next roll produces an 11, and you win again. Now you've got another $10 that you're paid off, so you've got $20. Our rule calls for taking one chip back—$5. (We always use the term *unit:* betting one unit—and when you win, you bet two units.) In this case our unit has been $5, but it could be $25 as well. Now you have three units riding on the line.

*   *   *

Now the shooter comes out with a 6 for a number. As we mentioned, you should always take the odds in back of your bet. So, you take $15 and put it in back of your $15 *line* bet. The roller rolls a couple of more times and then makes the 6. You now get paid $15 on the line which gives you six units there, and for your $15 *odds* bet which was in back of your $15 *line* bet you get paid $18—six dollars for each five. So now you pick up the $18, together with your $15 *odds* bet, but you let the $30 ride on the *pass line* because of, as we will show you after we finish this section, the method of doubling up called "progressive betting." You bet one, win; bet two, win; take one down and bet three. Now when you make your three bet, you have six, and we leave the six to ride. This is important because this is your biggest bet so far. The shooter comes out and shoots a 7. He makes a natural 7, and you've just won another $30 (or six units). Now the rule tells us that we bet four units and take down two units in net profits. So, out of your $60 you now have $60 going, you've won $30, and have twelve $5 units. So you're taking $40 back (eight units) and letting four units ride.

Your net profit off your *line* bets is now $40. In addition to the $18 won previously, you're now $58 ahead, minus the $20 loss, so you're actually $38 ahead.

Now let's say the shooter rolls a 9. You've got a $20 *pass line* bet, you take $20 and put it in back of your $20 *line* bet. The shooter rolls a few more numbers and then he comes back with a 9. You get paid $20 on the *line* giving you nine units or $40, and you get 30 to 20 on your odds bet, so you get $30 there, and you put this in your rack along with your $20 *odds* bet.

So, you're off to a good score, which continues like this. Any time you win on one unit, you bet two. Take your four units and take one down, betting three. Three units win on the line, you have six, you bet, you win and you have 12, you take down eight, you have four going.

* * *

Now the reason for this method of betting, instead of doubling-up on top of the other, is that we do not know in a chance game like craps or roulette if the next throw of the dice or turn of the wheel will give us a winner or loser. So if we hit on a "lucky streak," like the last hand, we don't know if it will continue. Never count on a lucky streak continuing, because you never can tell just when it will end. Every time another win comes, sure, it adds to the lucky streak. But you must always talk about a streak like this in retrospect, not trying to project it into the future, because we can not predict the future. So, make the most of your wins but use common sense. Leave enough on to take advantage of another win if you're lucky, but take something back in the event that you lose, so you still have some safe profits from the previous wins.

Let's say that on the next roll the shooter rolls a crap, ace-deuce. This is a loss, so you take back five units and play the original one unit, $5. Once you get a loss, you cannot make the same size bet or add anything. If you're wiped out on your *pass line* bet, you start all over with one unit. Same method: if that wins, you bet two; if that wins, you bet three; if that wins, you bet six; bet wins, you bet 4; wins, bet 5. You just keep repeating that form.

In this way, you are minimizing the amount you can lose and maximizing your wins while safeguarding them at the same time.

So here you are back to our single $5 one-unit bet. Now he shoots an 8, and you take five and put it in back of the 8, and the shooter rolls a 7, so you've lost the $5 *line* bet and the $5 odds in back; so when the next shooter comes up you put $5 on the line again. But you will see that if you count up, you're still ahead this way in spite of a few losses, because you have used this progressive betting system.

Remember: The formula is, bet 1, win; bet 2, win; bet 3, win; bet 6, win; bet 4 and take back 8. (See Diagram 10-1.) Conversely, if you had taken the $50 and lost it all, you would walk away knowing you have three other $50 playing sessions.

The Progressive Money Management System

Bet in units. A unit should be a one-chip denomination, such as $1, $5, $25. Conceivably, though, if you wanted your unit bets to be larger than $1 but not as much as $5, your unit bet could be $2 (two $1 chips). For the purpose of the chart, we're going to use $5 chips as our units, as we did in the previous example.

This time we will play our progressive money management method at the *roulette* table. Here you have a choice of betting even money situations and also areas in which you receive 2 to 1 for a winning wager. Each spin of the wheel gives you a win or lose decision. (You may wish to review Chapter 5 to refresh your memory of the roulette rules and table layout.)

* * *

According to the odds of roulette as it is played in the casinos of Nevada and Atlantic City, there are 38 selections around the wheel in which to bet. They are the numbers 1 through 36, 0 and 00. As stated, there are 38 slots identical in size and space around the wheel. The true probability of selecting one of these numbers is 1 in 38, or odds of 37 to 1. However, the casino needs a little edge and they pay 35 to 1. You put a $1 chip on a number and if it comes up on that spin of the wheel you get 35 to 1, or a total of $36. That gives the house a 5¼% edge, which is not the worst bet in the world; you pay 17% at the thoroughbred race tracks.

If you were to make 10,000 $1 bets on an even money bet such as red or black, and if the wheel showed an equal number of red as black, you'd lose $525 at the end of the 10,000 spins. The green 0 and 00 is the house edge, and they would show up just enough for you to lose 5¼% of your bankroll.

Of course, it's not likely that you'd see *exactly* 525 green numbers during any designated 10,000 roulette spins. But the house edge is a reality, and making flat bets (all the same denomination) will eventually whittle your bankroll down to nothing.

Therefore, if you are to win, you must bet progressively. Diagram 10-1 further explains and illustrates our progressive money management system. The betting formula is 1-2-3*-6-4**-8. (Bets are $5 units.)

Diagram 10-1

	Units Bet	Win	Lose	Cumulative Win–Loss
	1	1		+ 1
	2		2	– 1
start over	1		1	– 2
start over	1	1		– 1
	2	2		+ 1
* take 1 unit back	3	3		+ 4
let 6 ride	6	6		+ 10
* * take 8, let 4 ride	4		4	+ 6
start over; next bet is	1			

You advance your bets, making them progressively larger, when you win. But always go back to the original one-unit bet when a loss occurs. The idea of taking some profits off during the win sequence is one that ensures you will show some net profit on any win sequence. You continue to progressively advance your bets with each previous win.

The two-unit win bet gives you four units. However, you drag one unit, which was your original starting bet. You play the three units, and if it wins, let it ride. Then, when that wins, you take off eight units in profit, letting four units ride. The next bet would be the full eight units, and with a win there, you can move up to a 10-unit bet, dragging six units in profit.

In other words, if a really hot hand is unfolding, you want to be on it with progressively higher bets, yet taking profits along the way.

Putting Some Aside

When do you know if it's time to leave the crap table? Here is the rule: As soon as you have accumulated double your bankroll, put your original bankroll (say it's $50) off to one side of your chip rack, *where it's not to be touched again!* Now you're playing with the $50 in profits. You're using the money management plan that helped you win the $50 in the first place.

Suppose you get lucky and win another $50 with your $50 profits. You take another $50 and put it aside as you did with your original bankroll. This is just like putting it in your pocket. Each time you win another $50, you put it on the side or in your pocket to take with you. There is no way you can lose that money once it's put aside. If you ever lose the money that's in front of you, do not dip into your previous winnings to attempt to recoup. Leave that money alone once it's been put aside.

This philosophy tells us that as long as we continue to win back our original bankroll, we can continue to play in this session. This way, you can combine the thrill of winning with the security of knowing you won't walk away from the table a loser no matter what happens in your subsequent wagering. Most players don't have a method or formula like this to guide them. When they do win, they're good candidates for losing it all. This can't happen to you as long as you stick to this formula, because the temptation to pile chips on a winning bet without restraint is counteracted. In games of chance, remember that our "winning streak" or lucky cycle is only as good as the last win.

The beautiful part of this method of progressive betting is that for as long as you can gather those increments of $50 each time and put $50 in your pocket, you can continue to play in that session.

Once you get far enough ahead, you might want to take the risk of doubling up a whole roll, because you're only risking profits—some of them, not all. So whether you win or lose big on that particular roll, remember that you're still ahead of the game and you're protecting yourself.

Remember the Guidelines

Your goal is to keep building those $50 increments, and whenever you can do that, keep playing that session. Incidentally, you can always trade in $5 chips for $25 chips, or "green chips," to save space in your pocket or your rack. You leave the table when you lose the playing money in front of you. You *never* dip back into your previous wins in your pocket or the side of your rack to take out money once you've lost the amount in your current play. This way, you can walk away from the table a winner even if you've just lost all the money in your playing increment. You hope this won't happen, of course, but the idea is that even if it does, you can still walk away with the feeling of being "home free."

Once you're playing, the progressive system is working out beautifully, and you're beginning to amass some impressive winnings, you can switch from $5 units to $25 units. In that case, you've got to go in with about $200, eight $25 chips, but *the same rules apply.* You're just moving up in the world! Using these principles, you can go from winning hundreds to winning thousands. But—it's worth repeating: *stick to the principles set forth here.* *Never* increase your bets on a previous loss. *Always* increase your bets on a previous win (only with winning chips that the dealer has paid you). The same principles work for the Wheel of Fortune, baccarat, or any game of chance. Don't forget to use these principles in all eight playing sessions.

Remember that this philosophy—as well as your own discipline in adhering to it—will serve you well in any game of chance, at any betting level. Good luck, and win big!

Chapter 11
Gaming Tournaments:
Learning the Rules and Requirements

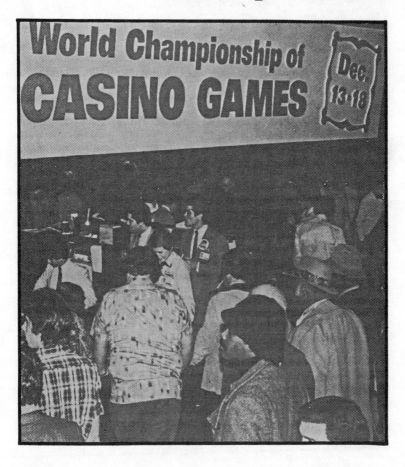

Casino-sponsored gaming tournaments are relatively new on the gambling scene, be they in Vegas, Reno, Tahoe or Atlantic City. For the longest time, visitors came to these resorts mainly to play the usual casino games. But now the hotels have a lot of competition with each other, and must tempt visitors with something new. Thus, tournaments came into being.

Poker

Actually, for the past ten years, there *have* been poker tournaments, the most notable being the World Series of Poker sponsored by Binion's Horseshoe Casino in downtown Las Vegas. Today this is a million-dollar tournament in which all kinds of poker games are played over a period of about four weeks. They start off with smaller pots like $25 to $100,000, moving all the way up to a $1 million game. This has brought in many crack poker players from all over the country, because the contestants get a good break when they enter the tournaments. It's very festive, attracts a lot of spectators, and the sponsoring hotel is giving something to the tournaments. For example, in Binion's all the entry fees go into the pot to be won by the players. In some cases the entry fee is $10,000. Binion's is profiting only from the publicity they will receive by sponsoring the tournament and providing the arena for this impressive contest.

The other well known tournament, the Amarillo Slim Super Bowl of Poker conducted at the Sahara Tahoe casino-resort, is much like Binion's. There are many other smaller poker tournaments going on throughout the year, attracting the most skillful players from every state and even from other countries such as England, Ireland, and France.

For the astute player, or for the player who feels he is a bit beyond average (the best, perhaps, in his own group at home), these tournaments are a real boon. In such tournaments sometimes even amateur players can walk away with a lot of money.

Blackjack

In the past five years, one casino game that has become a very popular tournament game is blackjack, or "21." This game is particularly big with younger gamblers, people in their 20s and 30s, who've learned that there is a way of playing blackjack, a certain strategy involved, which makes it somewhat a game of skill. In tournaments the players compete with each other, as well as with the house (as in roulette, craps, etc.). Here's how it works.

First of all, there are time limits on the tournaments (or a fixed number of hands to be played: 100) as well as restrictions on how much money is used. You will be eliminated from the competition or the round if and when you lose the original amount which you have bought in for. You cannot replenish losses with fresh money; once the initial amount is lost—whether it be $500, $700, or whatever—the player is out.

The time limit is usually two hours to a playing session in a blackjack tournament. In two hours you can't really put together any great playing technique, especially when you're playing against the house and your fellow contestants at the table. So, luck and timing prevail in these tournaments.

"Anyone 21 years or older can enter the $35,000 Sands International Blackjack Open. A registration fee and buy-in of $600 will be required of each contestant."

Thus reads the entry guidelines of the Sands International Blackjack Open. The players, seated together at random, are required to bet each hand with a minimum bet of five dollars and a maximum bet of $500. Even if someone has amassed chips totaling two or three thousand dollars, the limit that person could bet would still be $500.

* * *

The object is to beat the dealer *and* the other players seated around the table. There is one winner per table; the player who wins Round 1 at the table advances to Round 2. The players who lose Round 1 are out of the game, unless—and this is a recent amendment—they wish to pay another registration fee and begin again. The winner is not required to pay any additional fee. There are sometimes prizes awarded to the winners of the round.

Round 2 continues much as Round 1, with the same betting limits and rules. Players must keep their chips visible to the other players. At the end of the two-hour play, the person with the most chips is declared the winner. (In the Sands competition, exactly 100 hands are dealt, which amounts to about two hours, and a break in-between.) In the Sands tournament, a maximum of six players are seated at a table.

At the end of a round, each player gets to keep the chips in front of him or her. So even if the other five players at the table are deemed losers of the round, they may still be ahead if they each finish with more than $600, which was the entry fee. At the end of the round, the chips are cashed in, because they are not good for any other game in the casino.

At the end of Round 3, the winners are in what is called the Championship Playoff, and eligible to win as much as $75,000 in cash. That winner will be awarded the title of Sands International Blackjack Open Champion. A beautiful trophy goes along with this award, as well as a considerable amount of prestige.

The winners of Rounds 1, 2 and 3 receive bonus prizes of $25,000, $40,000 and $60,000 respectively, and nine runner-up prizes are awarded. These include complimentary accommodations in the Sands Hotel in either Vegas, Tahoe or Puerto Rico. Also, the player who accumulates the highest number of total winnings in all three rounds is awarded the title of Cumulative Winner and automatically advances to the Championship Playoff. Even if this player did not win any preliminary round, if his *total* winnings in all three rounds are higher than anybody else's, he wins the privilege of playing in the championship round.

Staying Informed

Anyone with an eye toward the big jackpot of a tournament should send away to the appropriate hotel or sponsoring casino

Chapter 11

for a rules brochure and read it over carefully. The rules are fairly easy to understand and therefore these tournaments attract a wide variety of people from all over; they provide an excellent opportunity to meet people in an exciting, high-rolling atmosphere.

These tournaments provide a great deal of fun and excitement for the few days of their duration, and provide a lot of opportunity for players to win money and prizes. In the Sands Contest last year, the Cumulative Winner was awarded a 1982 Cadillac. There are many other exciting tournaments in addition to the Sands', including those held at the Sahara, Riviera, and Tropicana hotels. By reading publications such as *Gambling Times* magazine, one can keep abreast of the various tournaments, rules and dates.

Craps

Craps tournaments are also very popular these days. The entrants are required to post a $250 entry fee, some of which is funneled into the prize pots.

Again, the table assignments for each player are randomly selected, with each player given an arbitrary number. The craps game is played the conventional way (see Chapter 1) with 12 to 14 players assigned to each table. There is one round per hour. When the hour is up, whoever has the dice—the shooter—may finish his roll. The round does not end until that particular shoot is through.

Players must keep their chips in front of them, by denomination, in their racks. As in the blackjack tournaments, the minimum bet on a roll is $5, and the maximum is $500. On the proposition bets (like hard way 4, hard way 6, hard way 8 and hard way 10), 7, ace, ace-deuce, and 11, there is a $25 limit. On all other bets the limit is $500.

As in the blackjack tourneys, whoever wins Round 1 advances to Round 2. In some places, both the winner and the runner-up at each table may advance to the second round. Each player is given a receipt for his chips, which is cashed in at the end of the round. There are cash prizes awarded along the way to the winners of each round, as in the card tournaments.

Simple rules apply to the players: Keep your chips in view,

hands off the table, etc. Courtesy and fair play are the name of the game.

Other Tournaments

Another popular contest is the backgammon tournament. The Dunes runs a backgammon tournament which has been very successful for many years. This is a glamorous, exciting game well-loved by the international jet set. Timely information as to these tournament schedules can be obtained by writing to *Gambling Times* magazine.

Gin rummy is also played in tournaments nowadays, even though it is not a casino game, and enthusiasts of the game come from all over the country to play.

* * *

The gaming tournaments, aside from providing fun and excitement for the players, also serve to promote the hotels and casinos that host them. They help to bring new faces to the scene, people who will return at a later date for another vacation.

Wherever you decide to play, remember to obtain the schedule and rules well in advance, enter as early as possible, have fun, and, hopefully, good luck!

Chapter 12
Casino Gaming:
Other Games

This concluding chapter illustrates and explains the basics of two games not covered in this book in greater detail: Baccarat and the Wheel of Fortune.

When found in casinos, these games are usually few in number and receive the least amount of player participation, although baccarat is played for high stakes and usually represents significant swings in overall casino wins and losses.

The Basics of Baccarat

Simple and Elegant

The word "baccarat" is derived from the Italian *baccara*, which means zero. The term refers to the face cards and the 10, all of which have zero value in the game of baccarat. In Europe, baccarat and a similar version called *chemin de fer* are among the most popular casino games.

Since baccarat's inception in Nevada, the game has assumed a glamour look. In most casinos, baccarat is played in a separate, roped-off area. The intention was to attract the high roller, or the more sophisticated, moneyed player. With the tuxedo-clad dealers, there is an elegance and aloofness to the game.

* * *

However, for all its enchantment, baccarat is primarily a simplistic game. There are no decisions or options: no degree of skill is required for either player or dealer. Players may sit in any open seat at the table; seating position does not affect the play in any manner. Each seat corresponds to a number on the layout, 1 through 15. Three dealers service the table. The dealer standing between positions 1 and 15 is known as the *caller*. He runs the game as cards are dealt from the shoe.

Each player gets a turn to handle the shoe. The player must bet the bank when he has the shoe, but any player may decline the shoe and it passes right along from player to player. Again, there is no advantage or disadvantage in dealing the cards; it's merely a formality and part of the ambience that players enjoy.

The caller receives the cards from the player with the shoe, places them in the appropriate boxes, and then calls for another card, or declares the winner, according to the rigid rules of the game.

157

Betting

Players bet by placing their chips in the numbered box opposite their seat. Bets may be made on the player or bank, and both are paid off at even money. In most games, bets range from $20 minimum to $2000 maximum.

After the winner is announced, the two other dealers at the table pay off the winning bets and collect from the losers. If the *bank* was the winner, players who won must pay a 5% commission on their winnings. Thus, if a player had a $100 bet on the bank and it won, $5 would be owed to the house.

Rather than collect this vigorish after each game, a record of what is owed by each player is kept in a numbered box just opposite where the two payoff dealers sit. Players pay this accumulated amount after the finish of a *shoe*. Each time the shoe is depleted of cards, all eight decks are thoroughly shuffled and replaced in the shoe.

Determining the Value of the Hands

All cards, ace through 9, are valued according to their count. Tens and face cards count as zero. Thus, if the first two cards dealt are a king and a 4, the count is 4. An 8 and 6, although totaling 14, would come to 4 after subtracting 10. Here is a list of two-card and three-card totals to further illustrate the method of counting cards:

Cards	Hand Total
6, 5	1
4, 10	4
3, queen	3
8, 2	0
10, jack	0
9, king	9
8, 8	6
6, 4, 8	8
10, 4, 3	7
5, 2	7

When any two cards total over a 10 count, 10 must be subtracted. The remaining total is the card count.

Rules of Play

These rules apply in all American casinos. Printed copies of these rules are available wherever baccarat is played. Dealers act according to these rules without consulting players at the table. The rules are automatic.

The highest total any baccarat hand can have is 9. A two-card total of 9 is called a *natural* and cannot lose. An 8 is the second best hand and is also called a natural. If both player and bank are dealt identical hands, it's a *standoff* (a tie) and neither bank nor player wins.

No further cards can be drawn to a two-card draw of 6 or 7.

When holding other two-card totals, player and bank draw another card at the direction of the dealer who does the calling. In studying the printed chart, one can easily determine the rules of the game.

It's a matter of letting the dealer do the calling, and declaring the outcome. Players are concerned only with how much they wager on each hand, and whether they bet on the player's side, or the banker's. The house edge in baccarat is the lowest of any casino game. With only a 5% commission on winning bank bets, and nothing taken from winning player bets, the player's disadvantage is only 1.37%. In some casinos, ties are permitted to be bet on. The payoff is 8 to 1. It's a bad bet for the player as the house edge is 14.1%.

Mini-Baccarat

A number of casinos have installed smaller baccarat tables, usually in among the blackjack tables. It's the same game, but the rituals of passing the shoe, etc., are missing, and the game is staffed by one dealer. The layout, however, conforms to the regular baccarat table, and each seat position (1 through 6) corresponds to a numbered betting box. Limits are usually from a $2 to $5 minimum up to $500 maximum. Mini-baccarat is played fast, but the exact same rules apply as in the larger game.

RULES:

Player	When first two cards total:
1–2–3–4–5–10	Draws a card
6–7	Stands
8–9	Natural–Stands

Banker	When first two cards total:	
Having:	Draws when Player's third card is:	Does not draw when Player's third card is:
3	1–2–3–4–5–6–7–9–10	8
4	2–3–4–5–6–7	1–8–9–10
5	4–5–6–7	1–2–3–8–9–10
6	6–7	1–2–3–4–5–8–9–10
7	STANDS	
8–9	NATURAL—STANDS	

Baccarat Terminology

BANKER—The dealer hand in baccarat.

BANKER HAND—A bet that the hand called *banker* will come closer to 9 than the hand called *player.* Pays 1 to 1. A 5% fee is charged to all winning banker hands.

NATURAL—An 8 or 9 count in baccarat.

PLAYER—The player hand in baccarat.

PLAYER HAND—A bet that the hand called *player* will come closer to 9 than the hand called *banker*. Pays 1 to 1, with no commission charge.

PUSH—When hands tie in baccarat.

SHILL—A player employed by the casino who is usually at the baccarat table to help create the illusion of activity on an otherwise quiet table.

TALLY SHEETS—Slips of lined paper which enable players to keep a record of how hands are falling, and determine whether they are winning or losing.

TIE—A bet that both the banker and player hands will tie. Pays 8 to 1. All bets on banker or player are considered a push in the event of a tie.

The Basics of the Wheel of Fortune

The Wheel

The game is known as the Big Six, or the Wheel of Fortune. It's another easy-to-play casino attraction, reminiscent of the old carnival wheels.

The wheel itself is made of wood in an elaborate and colorful design. Approximately six feet in diameter, the wheel is divided into nine parts, each part consisting of six identically spaced slots. There are exactly 54 of these slots separated by metal studs.

Positioned at the top of the wheel is a leather flap, and when the wheel is turning, a tick, tick, tick sound is heard as the strap hits against the nail-like metal studs.

Finally, as the wheel slows down, the strap will settle in one slot, and that particular one out of 54 slots will be declared the winner.

Betting

The slots are divided as follows: 23 $1 slots; 15 $2 slots; eight $5 slots; four $10 slots; two $20 slots and two slots that are joker or casino design slots.

Each of the slots carries the design of American currency, a $1 bill, for example, in each of the 23 $1 slots spread around the wheel.

A glass-covered table set in front of the wheel is where players place their bets. Pieces of currency, one to match each of the denominations around the wheel, are represented on this betting table layout. Players place their bets on top of their selection. A bet on the $1 bill will pay $1 for an even-money return if the spin of the wheel results in the leather strap stopping in the $1 bill slot.

A bet on the $2 bill pays off at 2 to 1. The $5 winner gets 5 to 1, the $10 winner receives odds of 10 to 1, and 20 to 1 odds go to the lucky player who selected the $20 denomination (if the wheel should stop in either of the two slots marked with a $20 bill).

If the player selects one of the special designs or joker designate, the payoff is 40 to 1. Each of these 40 to 1 selections is an individual bet. In all, there are seven choices for making a bet.

Figuring the Odds

To calculate the percentage in favor of the casino, we multiply each payoff symbol by its dollar value, subtract that from the remaining total number of symbols, and divide by 54. The $1 symbol gives us 23 chances of winning against 31 chances to lose. This leaves eight divided by 54.

The casino edge is 14.8%. The 15 $2 slots versus the 39 other chances give the house an edge of 16.7%. The eight $5 symbols, paying 5 to 1 odds, give the house an edge of 11.1%.

The four $10 slots paying off at 10 to 1 give the house an advantage of 18.5%. The two $20 slots with odds of 20 to 1, still provide a built-in edge of 22.2% in favor of the casino. Either choice of a single bet on the joker or special design slot work to a 24% house advantage.

Other combinations of denominations on the wheel will produce different house advantages...but now you know how to calculate the odds.

* * *

The attraction to the Wheel of Fortune is the aspect of fun and games. Patrons walking through the casino stop to watch the wheel as it spins and ticks, then stay to play a few dollars to see if their lucky guess produces a winner.

KEEPING YOUR GAMING
KNOWLEDGE CURRENT

Now that you know how to play the games you will find in legal gambling establishments, it's important to keep abreast of the rapid and continuous changes and developments in this area. The best way to do that is with a subscription to *Gambling Times* magazine.

Over the past six years, readers of *Gambling Times* magazine have profited immensely. They have done so by using the information they have read each month. If that sounds like a simple solution to winning more and losing less, well it is! Readers look to *Gambling Times* for that very specific reason. And it delivers.

Gambling Times is totally dedicated to showing readers how to win more money in every form of legalized gambling. How much you're going to win depends on many factors, but it's going to be considerably more than the cost of a subscription.

WINNING AND MONEY

Winning, that's what *Gambling Times* is all about. And money, that's what *Gambling Times* is all about. Because winning and money go hand in hand.

Here's what the late Vince Lombardi, the famous football coach of the Green Bay Packers, had to say about winning:

"It's not a sometime thing. Winning is a habit. There is no room for second place. There is only one place in my game and that is first place. I have finished second twice in my time at Green Bay and I don't ever want to finish second again. The objective is to win—fairly, squarely, decently, by the rules—but to win. To beat the other guy. Maybe that sounds hard or cruel. I don't think it is. It is and has always been an American zeal to be first in anything we do, and to win, and to win and to win."

Mr. Lombardi firmly believed that being a winner is "man's finest hour." *Gambling Times* believes it is too, while being a loser is depressing, ego-deflating, expensive and usually very lonely. "Everyone loves a winner" may be a cliche, but it's true. Winners command respect and are greatly admired. Winners are also very popular and have an abundance of friends. You may have seen many a winner in a casino, with a bevy of girls surrounding him. . .or remember one who could get just about any girl he wanted.

Some of the greatest gamblers in the world also have strong views on what winning is all about. Here's what two of them have to say on the subject:

"To be a winner, a man has to feel good about himself and know he has some kind of advantage going in. I never made bets on even chances. Smart is better than lucky."—"Titanic" Thompson

"When it comes to winnin', I got me a one-track mind. You gotta want to win more than anything else. And you gotta have confidence. You can't pretend to have it. That's no good. You gotta have it. You gotta know. Guessers are losers. Gamblin's just as simple as that."—Johnny Moss

Gambling Times will bring you the knowledge you need to come home a winner and come home in the money. For it is knowledge, the kind of knowledge you'll get in its pages, that separates winners from losers. It's winning and money that *Gambling Times* offers you. *Gambling Times* will be your working manual to winning wealth.

The current distribution of this magazine is limited to selected newsstands in selected cities. Additionally, at newsstands where it is available, it's being snapped up, as soon as it's displayed, by gamblers who know a sure bet when they see one.

So if you're serious about winning, you're best off subscribing to *Gambling Times*. Then you can always count on its being there, conveniently delivered to your mailbox—and what's more, it will be there one to two weeks before it appears on the newsstands. You'll be among the first to receive the current issue as soon as it comes off the presses, and being first is the way to be a winner.

Having every monthly issue of *Gambling Times* will enable you to build an "Encyclopedia of Gambling," since the contents of this magazine is full of sound advice that will be as good in five or ten years as it is now.

As you can see, a subscription to *Gambling Times* is your best bet for a future of knowledgeable gambling. It's your ticket to *WINNING* and *MONEY*.

Take the time to read the following offer. As you can see, *Gambling Times* has gone all out to give you outstanding bonuses. You can join the knowledgeable players who have learned that *Gambling Times* helps them to win more money.

FOUR NEW WAYS TO GET 12 WINNING ISSUES OF *GAMBLING TIMES* FREE.....

Every month over 250,000 readers trust *Gambling Times* to introduce powerful new winning strategies and systems. Using proven scientific methods, the world's leading experts show you how to win big money in the complex field of gambling.

Gambling Times has shown how progressive slot machines can be beat. Readers have discovered important new edges in blackjack. They've been shown how to know for sure when an opponent is bluffing at poker. *Gambling Times* has also spelled out winning methods for football, baseball and basketball. They've published profound new ways of beating horses. Their team of experts will uncover information in the months ahead that's certain to be worth thousands of dollars to you.

In fact, the features are so revolutionary that they must take special precautions to make sure *Gambling Times* readers learn these secrets long before anyone else. So how much is *Gambling Times* worth to you? Well...

NOW *GAMBLING TIMES* CAN BE BETTER THAN FREE! Here's how: This BONUS package comes AUTOMATICALLY TO YOU WHEN YOU SUBSCRIBE...or goes to a friend if you give a gift subscription.

(1) POKER BONUS at the TROPICANA card room in Las Vegas. Play poker at the TROPICANA and receive a free dinner buffet and comps to the "Folies Bergere" show for you *and* a guest. Value exceeds $40 excluding gratuities.

(2) FREE SPORTS BET. CHURCHILL DOWNS SPORTS BOOK in Las Vegas will let you make one wager up to $300 with no "vigorish." This means instead of laying the usual 11-to-10 odds, you can actually bet even up! You can easily save $30 here.

(3) PAYOFF BIGGER THAN THE TRACK. LEROY'S RACE BOOK, in Las Vegas, will add 10% to your payoff (up to $30 extra) on a special bet. Just pick the horse and the race of your choice, anywhere in America. For the first time in history, you can win more than the track pays.

(4) OUTSTANDING ROOM DISCOUNTS available only to *Gambling Times* subscribers. Check in at the SANDS in Las Vegas or Atlantic City, the TROPICANA in Atlantic City or the CONDADO INN & CASINO in San Juan, Puerto Rico. Stay for 3 days and 2 nights and you'll save $29 off their normal low rates.

THAT'S A SAVING EQUAL TO THE ENTIRE COST OF YOUR SUBSCRIPTION.

USE ALL FOUR CERTIFICATES (VALID FOR ONE YEAR)...GET *GAMBLING TIMES* FREE...AND YOU'LL PUT $90 IN YOUR POCKET!

To begin your delivery of *Gambling Times* magazine at once, enclose a payment of $29.00 by check or money order (U.S. currency), MasterCard or Visa. Add $5.00 per year for postage outside the United States.

Send payment to:

GAMBLING TIMES MAGAZINE
Dept. CG
1018 N. Cole Avenue
Hollywood, California 90038

GAMBLING TIMES
MONEY BACK GUARANTEE

If at any time you decide *Gambling Times* is not for you, you will receive a full refund on all unmailed copies. You are under no obligation and may keep the bonus as a gift.

OTHER BOOKS AVAILABLE

Other *Gambling Times* books include:

Big Winners' System Book—Contains 48 complete strategies for casino games and sports wagering, as well as several unique money management ideas that are absolutely vital to your gaming success. Features contributions from experts in their fields who achieve the proper balance between basic systems and material designed for career-oriented players. Covers blackjack, craps, keno, poker, roulette, horse racing, and sports betting (football, baseball, basketball). Softbound. (ISBN: 0-89746-021-9)

The Gambling Times Guide to Craps by N.B. Winkless, Jr.—The ultimate craps book for beginners and experts alike. It provides you with a system to beat the house edge that can be used on a home computer. This text shows you which bets to avoid and tells you the difference between craps in Nevada and craps in other gaming resort areas. It includes a glossary of terms and a directory of dealer schools. Softbound. (ISBN: 0-89746-013-8)

The Gambling Times Guide to Gaming Around the World—A compendium of major forms of legal gambling throughout the world, covering every country from Argentina to Zimbabwe. Tells you where to find casinos, card rooms, greyhound racing, horse racing, jai alai frontons, lotteries, and race and sports betting. Also discusses the basics of all these gaming activities. An exhaustive and definitive directory of world-wide gaming. Softbound. (ISBN: 0-89746-020-6)

Gambling Times on...Jai Alai by William R. Keevers—The most comprehensive book on jai alai available. Author Bill Keevers takes the reader on an informative journey from the ancient beginnings of the game to its current popularity. This easy-to-understand guide will show you the fine points of the game, how to improve your betting percentage, and where to find jai alai frontons. Softbound. (ISBN: 0-89746-010-3)

Million Dollar Blackjack by Ken Uston— Every blackjack enthusiast or gaming traveler who fancies himself a "21" player can improve his game with this explosive bestseller. Ken Uston shows you how he and his team won over 4 million dollars at blackjack. Now, for the first time, you can find out how he did it and how his system can help you. Includes playing and betting strategies, winning secrets, protection from cheaters, Uston's Advanced Point Count System, and a glossary of inside terms used by professionals. Hardbound. (ISBN: 0-914314-08-4)

P$yching Out Vegas by Marvin Karlins, Ph.D.—The dream merchants who build and operate gaming resorts subtly work on the casino patron to direct his attention, control his actions and turn his pockets inside out. At last, their techniques are revealed to you by a noted psychologist who shows you how you can successfully control your behavior and turn a losing attitude into a lifetime winning streak. Hardbound. (ISBN: 0-914314-03-3)

Winning Systems—A compilation of the best of *Gambling Times* magazine. Covering a period of six years, it features 14 all-inclusive gaming systems and betting methods. Includes chapters on craps, blackjack, roulette, keno, sports betting, and horse racing. Presented in an easy-to-understand style. Softbound. (ISBN: 0-89746-004-9)